EXPERIENCE

TOKYO

◎ Walking Eye App

YOUR FREE DESTINATION CONTENT AND EBOOK AVAILABLE THROUGH THE WALKING EYE APP

Your guide now includes a free eBook and destination content for your chosen destination, all for the same great price as before.
Simply download the Walking Eye App from the App Store or Google Play to access your free eBook and destination content.

HOW THE WALKING EYE APP WORKS

Through the Walking Eye App, you can purchase a range of eBooks and destination content. However, when you buy this book, you can download the corresponding eBook and destination content for free. Just see below in the grey panels where to find your free content and then scan the QR code at the bottom of this page.

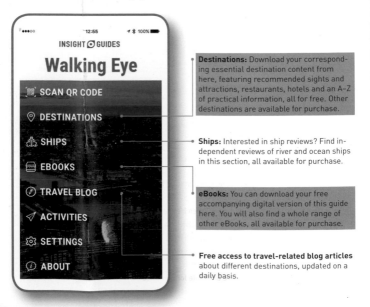

Destinations: Download your corresponding essential destination content from here, featuring recommended sights and attractions, restaurants, hotels and an A–Z of practical information, all for free. Other destinations are available for purchase.

Ships: Interested in ship reviews? Find independent reviews of river and ocean ships in this section, all available for purchase.

eBooks: You can download your free accompanying digital version of this guide here. You will also find a whole range of other eBooks, all available for purchase.

Free access to travel-related blog articles about different destinations, updated on a daily basis.

CONTENTS

HOW THE DESTINATION CONTENT WORKS

Each destination includes a short introduction, an A–Z of practical information and recommended points of interest, split into 4 different categories:

• Highlights
• Accommodation
• Eating out
• What to do

You can view the location of every point of interest and save it by adding it to your Favourites. In the 'Around Me' section you can view all the points of interest within 5km.

HOW THE EBOOKS WORK

The eBooks are provided in EPUB file format. Please note that you will need an eBook reader installed on your device to open the file. Many devices come with this as standard, but you may still need to install one manually from Google Play.

The eBook content is identical to the content in the printed guide.

HOW TO DOWNLOAD THE WALKING EYE APP

1. Download the Walking Eye App from the App Store or Google Play.
2. Open the app and select the scanning function from the main menu.
3. Scan the QR code on this page – you will then be asked a security question to verify ownership of the book.
4. Once this has been verified, you will see your eBook and destination content in the purchased ebook and destination sections, where you will be able to download them.

Other destination apps and eBooks are available for purchase separately or are free with the purchase of the Insight Guide book.

TOKYO
OVERVIEW

After decades of sailing under the radar, the word is out. Arrivals figures are sky rocketing as Tokyo experiences an unprecedented tourism boom and the city sheds its modesty: Governor Yuriko Koike now wants Japan's capital to become the world's number one destination.

And with good reason. Tokyo's blend of traditional and hypermodern, its serene shrines and pulsing nightlife, its mouth-watering cuisine, punctilious service and pleasingly good value – and most of all the endless surprises that lie around every corner – have put it atop the contemporary traveller's list of must-see cities.

This is the city from which the world's oldest imperial line rules from a hidden palace over one of the planet's proudest peoples. Yet it's also the place that gave us Sony and anime, Hello Kitty and bullet trains, and a city that's continuously reinventing itself after being destroyed twice in the 20th century.

From the sushi vendors of Tsukiji fish market to the maids at Akihabara's *otaku* ('fanboy') cafés, from the chic boutiques of Shibuya to the scruffy bars of Shinjuku, this giant 13+ million-strong city in a sprawling megalopolis is opening its arms ever-wider to overseas visitors. And yet, even with the 2020 Summer Olympics bringing a building boom that's transforming the skyline, Tokyo remains tethered to a rich and ancient culture that keeps it a place of eternal fascination.

So get off the beaten path, venture down the narrow lanes that define residential Tokyo and discover a city that's not so far evolved from its past as a wide plain of verdant rice paddies, ringed by mountains and the sea - occupied by sturdy folk who, by dint of hard work and resourceful creativity, lofted Japan to its spot as the world's third-biggest economy.

IN THE MOOD FOR...

... A FOODIE EXTRAVAGANZA

Tokyo is a perfect foodie paradise. With one of the world's most renowned native cuisines, and the most Michelin stars of any city on earth, Tokyo serves up some exceptional dishes that you'll remember for a lifetime.

Japan's capital isn't only about multi-course menus or haute cuisine. There's also an abundance of earthier delights along the lines of the cattail-shaped, pan-fried donuts you'll find at **Shipoya** or 'tail shop' in Yanaka (see page 129), a haven for what the Japanese call 'B-grade gourmet'. You'll also find plenty of hearty and unpretentious dishes, like its famous ramen noodles – slurp them up at Ebisu's **Afuri** (see page 83). For *nabe* and *sukiyaki* (hot-pot dishes), head to Ryogoku's centuries-old **Momonjiya** (see page 149), which makes them from venison and even bear meat.

Tsukiji fish market (see page 40) is a vital stop on the Tokyo sight-seeing trail, where you can observe auctions, buy kitchenware and tuck into the planet's freshest sushi. And if your sushi dreams still aren't sated, go high-tech and have your sushi whizzed to you on mini Shinkansen trains at conveyer-belt sushi spot **Katsu Midori** (see page 70) in Shibuya. Equally central to Japanese cuisine is rice, and you can experience the freshest, tastiest rice in the city at Yoyogi's serene **Ohitsuzen Tanbo** (see page 81), which grows its own. Indulge in their carefully crafted *onigiri* (rice balls) and grilled fish sets.

Head to Roppongi's three-star restaurant **Ryugin** (see page 61) if you're prepared to really splash out, where chef Seiji Yamamoto specialises in *kaiseki ryori* – multi-course meals conjured from the finest ingredients from across the Japanese archipelago.

Themed spots abound in a city where people view dining as a fun experience to be savoured for hours with flowing drinks and conversation. Try Akasaka's **Ninja Restaurant** (see page 43), where masked ninja lead you to your table in 'The Village' through a web of hidden doors.

... RETAIL THERAPY

Tokyo is pricy, but no more so than any other megalopolis – and the service is punctilious to a fault. Go upscale at swish department stores like Ginza's **Wako** (see page 34) and **Mitsukoshi** (see page 34), or follow the trendsetters to temples of youth-culture fashion such as Shibuya's **Movida** (see page 71) or Harajuku's **Laforet** (see page 101).

If you prefer small boutiques, eschew the department stores to stroll around **Daikanyama** (see page 101), one of Tokyo's smartest districts and home to shops featuring the creations of Japan's top designers.

Lovely handmade crafts from across the archipelago are available at **Bingoya** (see page 108) near Shinjuku, while **Yanaka** (see page 129), the Tsukiji **Outer Market** (see page 40) and Asakusa's **Senso-ji** (see page ?) are all excellent for traditional bric-a-brac.

For J-pop culture, make for **Tower Records** (see page 68) in Shibuya; for ('fanboy') goods like anime and manga and high-tech gadgets are ?, **Akihabara** (see page 130) is the place. **Kiddy Land** (see page ? course – the temple for all things toy-like.

... A NIGHT ON THE TOWN

By night, Tokyoites put aside strict formalities and let loose. From your local *izakaya* (food-and-drinks bar) to cutting-edge nightclubs and dingy hostess bars, there's something for everyone.

For expats, nightlife begins with a pub crawl in **Roppongi** (see page 58), where you can hang out with traders at places like **Wall Street**. Alternatively, mingle with 'new half' transsexual entertainers at **Kingyo Club** (see page 55) or experimental-minded hipsters at **SuperDeluxe** (see page 60).

If you're into bass 'n' beats, Shibuya is the place to go. The party doesn't stop until past the crack of dawn as world-class DJs play at clubs like **Sound Museum Vision, Womb** and **Contact** (see page 69).

Golden Gai (see page 106) in Shinjuku offers an intriguing mix of the historic and contemporary. Here, in what are little more than shacks thrown up in the wake of World War II, enterprising proprietors have fashioned a welter of tiny bars that range from temple of pop culture **Bar Plastic Model** to **Tachibana 'examination room'**, where bartenders prepare cocktails with names like 'Colonic Irrigation'.

... FAMILY FUN

With its whizzing trains, neon lights and electronic noises, the capital is a wonderland for kids – and that's before you've hit **Disneyland** and **Disney Sea** (see page 156) in suburban Chiba.

Disney isn't the only amusement park in Tokyo. For nostalgia buffs there's Japan's oldest amusement park, **Hanayashiki** (see page 140) in Asakusa, while **Odaiba** (see page 154) offers a Sega game centre, Ferris Wheel and all manner of family entertainment. For fans of anime-legend Hayao Miyazaki, a visit to his **Ghibli Museum** (see page 157) is a must, before relaxing in Inokashira Koen Park.

On the educational front, Tokyo has several excellent museums for a day's outing. With its giant real-time rotating globe and robot show, the cutting-edge **National Museum of Emerging Science and Innovation** (see page 165) will delight visitors both young and old, as will the **Edo-Tokyo Museum** (see page 145) with its historic scale replicas.

And don't miss the activities. Kids and adults can become warriors at the **Samurai Training Experience** (see page 138), master the essentials of sushi preparation at the **Tokyo Sushi Academy** (see page 44) or discover the real Tokyo by bike with **Freewheeling Japan** (see page 160).

... TEMPLES, SHRINES AND PALACES

Tokyo, the most hyper-modern of cities, also boasts numerous Shinto shrines and Buddhist temples, oases of spirituality amidst Japan's unapologetic commercialism. **Meiji-jingu** (see page 92), near Harajuku, is not only a gracious wooden shrine and one of Tokyo's largest green spaces, it's also where you can experience a 1000-year-old Shinto blessing ritual for yourself.

In Asakusa, **Senso-ji** (see page 139) is Tokyo's oldest Buddhist temple and an ancient pilgrimage spot. The approach is lined with 80 shops where you can pick up anything from traditional textiles and Buddhist scrolls to a Hello Kitty-themed accessory for your mobile phone.

On Tokyo's outskirts are districts where historic structures have been left undamaged by the firebombing of Tokyo during World War II. **Kamakura** (see page 158) was the shogun's 14th-century capital and is now a leafy suburb where giant Buddhas share space with chic restaurants. Mount Takao, on the other hand, offers verdant trails, atmospheric temples and a charming souvenir village.

Finally, don't leave Tokyo without visiting the stately **Imperial Palace** (see page 28), home to the world's oldest monarchy.

... TRADITIONAL CULTURE

Despite its newcomer status as capital, Tokyo can claim as much traditional culture as Kyoto. Here, you'll find the **Kabuki-za** (see page 32),
where you can absorb a performance of the stylised theatre form *Kabuki*.
(Tokyo also hosts a National Theatre and Noh Theatre for other traditional
performing arts.)

Japan's refined tea ceremony can also be experienced in the capital. The **Hamarikyu Garden** (see page 37) offers a do-it-yourself tea
ceremony, while **Omotenashi Nihonbashi** (see page 45) hosts a 'Time
To Geisha' programme in which guests are entertained for an hour as
geishas dance and sing to the piquant *shamisen* (a banjo-like instrument).
With tourism on the rise in Tokyo, a number of similar programmes now
cater to the foreign fascination with geisha.

Tokyo is also the capital of sumo, with three of six tournaments held
at the **Ryogoku Kokugikan arena** (see page 146) each year. Even if the
stars don't align, it's possible to watch the giants clash in a morning
practice at a sumo stable.

... THE ARTS

Tokyo has a busy contemporary art scene, but exploration should begin with the nation's own rich artistic tradition. The best place to do this is the **Tokyo National Museum** (see page 122), home to a mother-load of traditional objects ranging from sublime paintings to *ukiyo-e* woodblock prints that provide a visual narrative to Japan's thousands of years of history.

The serene **Nezu Museum** (see page 97) in Aoyama is another excellent place to take in national treasures in genres spanning calligraphy to ceramics, bamboo crafts to textiles. If you're seeking something intimate, this is the spot.

Contemporary art hounds can choose from a growing number of venues. Start with a tour of **Ginza's galleries** (see page 41) and then head to one of Tokyo's several excellent new museums. High atop Roppongi Hills, the **Mori Art Museum** (see page 50) boasts some of the most forward-thinking curators found anywhere in the world, while the **Museum of Contemporary Art, Tokyo** (see page 141) houses a first-rate collection in an imposing rectilinear building.

... *KAWAII*, *OTAKU* AND J-POP CULTURE

Japan is no longer just about cars and high-tech, it's a cultural powerhouse.

Kawaii ('cute') and offbeat fashions emanating from Harajuku make this a must-see district. For boutique browsing, **Urahara** (see page 88) is a wonderful warren of funky clothing and accessories shops, while the nearby **Kawaii Monster Cafe** (see page 100) packages *kawaii* culture into an eating, dining and entertainment experience.

If you're after gaming, manga and anime, head to *otaku* ('fanboy') ground central **Akihabara** (see page 127). Here you'll find a dizzying array of gaming shops, manga temple **Mandarake** and Japan's biggest retail chain for anime goods, **Animate**.

J-pop fans should make a beeline for Shibuya's **Tower Records** (see page 68). This vast emporium holds 800,000 items in stock over seven floors. Should you be in the mood to sing yourself, a visit to a 'karaoke box' like the lavish **Karaoke Pasera Resort** (see page 73) is in order.

... OFFBEAT EXPLORATION

Getting off the beaten track reveals a whole different Tokyo. Ride a bike with **Freewheeling Japan** (see page 160) through the back alleys and unfrequented shrines of residential Tokyo. Or head out of the city centre to **Koenji** (see page 162), where you'll find Tokyo's hippest suburb and a plethora of cafés, boutiques and 'live house' music clubs. Take the train for an hour to wind up at the foot of sacred **Mount Takao** (see page 161), a paradise of forest paths, temples and quaint noodle shops.

... PEOPLE WATCHING

On a weekend, there's no better place for observing Tokyo's varied population than **Yoyogi Park** (see page 91), where you can relax amid the greenery and even enjoy street entertainment. The rooftop cafés and bars atop the nearby **Tokyu Plaza Omotesando Harajuku** (see page 99), meanwhile, offer the perfect perch from which to observe the thronging avenue below.

... ROMANCE

Tokyo Tower (see page 52) and **Tokyo Skytree** (see page 144) are ideal spots to watch the sun set over a glittering skyline. For a dinner date, you couldn't do much better than booking a table at the **Marubiru** (see page 33), with a view across to Tokyo Station. If it's nightlife you're after, take in a show at the swanky **Billboard Live TOKYO** (see page 51) in nearby Roppongi.

... JAPANESE HIGH-TECH

Two vast science museums, the **National Museum of Emerging Science and Innovation** (see page 165) and the **National Museum of Nature and Science** (see page 132), offer a spectrum of insights into Japan's technical expertise. Riding the driverless Yurikamome line or even walking across via **Rainbow Bridge** (see page 154) to Odaiba offers you visions of the future as you head to a gaming and shopping paradise.

... STREET LIFE

Shibuya and its famous **Scramble Crossing** (see page 71) are legendary for their street life, and a stroll up Center Gai towards **Yoyogi Park** (see page 91) offers a superb sample of 21st-century Tokyo bustle. **Kabukicho** (see page 106) comes alive with denizens of the night, while the cultural oasis that is **Ueno Park** (see page 122) is more salubrious. The nearby **Ameyoko street market** (see page 131) and **Yanaka Ginza** (see page 129) allow a glimpse of old Tokyo.

... ESCAPING THE CROWDS

Finding solitude in Tokyo can be a challenge, particularly on weekends, but you're likely to find peace and quiet at the **Chinzanso garden** (see page 113) almost anytime. On weekdays, **Yoyogi Park** (see page 91) and adjacent **Meiji-jingu** (see page 92) are islands of serenity, while the high-tech multimedia **NTT InterCommunication Center** (see page 112) and **National Art Center, Tokyo** (see page 63) are often surprisingly empty.

NEIGHBOURHOODS

With 23 wards, Tokyo follows a vague wheel-and-spokes plan, with the Yamanote line encompassing the city centre. Commuter lines branch off the Yamanote, and two roads – the inner Meiji-dori and outer Yamate-dori – also circle the city. However, Tokyo is mostly a crazy welter of alleys that grew from paths between rice paddies, and GPS systems are indispensable.

The Imperial Palace and Central Tokyo. The area around the Imperial Palace is both the symbolic centre of Japan as the home of its emperors, and the political centre of the country in the National Diet (parliament) and ministry buildings. Many powerful corporations have their headquarters nearby.

Roppongi and Akasaka. Roppongi and Akasaka developed mainly in the 20th century as the capital exploded in size. Long the centre of expat Tokyo, Roppongi boasts the nightlife district around Roppongi Crossing and the new Roppongi Art Triangle. Akasaka has more business and government buildings, but also enjoys a large nightlife area.

Shibuya and Ebisu. Shibuya's famous Scramble Crossing is the epicentre of Japan's youth-culture explosion, with the station area encompassing the country's top nightclubs, live-music spaces, cafés, boutiques, department stores and record shops. The buzz spills over to the more adult-oriented Ebisu, with trendy Dainkanyama in between.

Harajuku, Omotesando and Aoyama. Harajuku brings Shibuya youth culture to the north in a less built-up context, with Yoyogi Park providing a major escape valve from the city's pressures. Tree-lined Omotosando is often called 'Tokyo's Champs-Élysées', while Aoyama is defined by elegant residences, media firms and fashionable boutiques and cafés.

Shinjuku and Ikebukuro. Serving Tokyo's western and northern suburbs, Shinjuku Station is the world's busiest commuter hub. East of the station are the red-light district of Kabukicho, the atmospheric drinking area Golden Gai and gay hub Shinjuku Ni-chome; to the west is an office and museums area. Ikebukuro to the north offers a similar, if less impressive, mix of commerce, offices and nightlife.

Ueno, Yanaka and Akihabara. With several large museums, temples, a zoo and a performing arts centre, Ueno Park is Tokyo's main high culture district. Nearby, historic Yanaka was one of the few areas to survive the World War II firebombing, while Akihabara is a gadget centre and ground zero for Japan's *otaku* ('fanboy') scene.

Asakusa and East Tokyo. Asakusa was once the centre of Tokyo's old downtown area, and still contains the city's oldest Buddhist temple, Senso-ji, and its lively market. Crossing the Sumida River one finds East Tokyo district Ryogoku, the capital of sumo, and further south the Kiba area, home to the Museum of Contemporary Art, Tokyo.

Beyond the City Centre. Thirteen million people live in Tokyo proper, but the metropolitan area holds over 30 million. Built on reclaimed land, Tokyo Bay's Odaiba is a vision of the future. West of the city centre you'll find trendy suburbs like Koenji, while even further out there are mountain ranges including the historic Mount Takao. Heading southwest along the Pacific you'll reach the historic port city, Yokohama, and the leafy ancient capital, Kamakura.

THE IMPERIAL PALACE AND CENTRAL TOKYO

Stroll around Tokyo Castle, loadstone of Japanese tradition and power

An early morning visit to **Tokyo (Edo) Castle**, when the crows are cawing and joggers circuit the outer grounds, is the perfect way to experience this iconic fortress. Begun in 1590 by the Shogun

A dying line?

Japan's imperial line, said to have begun in 660 BC with the mythic Emperor Jimmu, is now in danger of dying out. Crown Prince Naruhito and Princess Masako have only one daughter, but Japan's laws only allow for a male heir, meaning that after Naruhito dies the Chrysanthemum Crown goes to young Prince Hisahito, the son of Naruhito's brother Akishino, and the only male grandson of Emperor Akihito. If Hisahito fails to produce a male offspring, Japan would then either have to allow for female succession – unthinkable to conservatives – or again open the line to cousins and the wider family, as in times past. (Imperial concubines, once a convenient way of ensuring male heirs, would of course be unacceptable in contemporary Japan). Japanese policymakers are kicking this uncomfortable political football into the future, but a wide range of opinions exist and many seek to open succession to women, notwithstanding the Emperor's key function in male-centric Shinto rituals.

Tokugawa Ieyasu, the castle includes – within its precincts – the **Imperial Palace** (Kokyo), home to Emperor Akihito, Empress Michiko, their children and grandchildren. Japan's imperial line is the longest on the planet; its emperors are said to be descended from the mythical sun goddess Amaterasu, a principal deity of the Shinto religion.

Walk through the **Kitahanebashi Gate** (Kitahanebashi-mon) to enter the **Imperial Palace East Garden** (Kokyo Higashi Gyoen), the site of Edo's original five-roofed keep. The keep burnt to the ground in 1657, but it is worth climbing the base to view the scenic surroundings. The massive stone walls of the inner moat testify to the immense wealth and power of the shoguns who unified Japan and moved the capital here from Kyoto. Huge blocks were hauled by ship from Izu, some 50 miles (80km) away.

Exit the garden through the charming, whitewashed **Ote Gate** (Ote-mon), a copy of the original main gate, and step into the Outer Garden, now known as the **Imperial Palace Plaza** (Kokyomae Hiroba). The former gardens,

planted with Japanese black pine trees and lawns in 1899, are bisected by Uchibori-dori road.

Continue south across the plaza and take a selfie against the striking backdrop of the **Double Layer Bridge** (Nijubashi), with the elegant **Fushimi Turret** (Fushimi Yagura), and perhaps a swan or two floating under the willow trees of the outer moat.

Follow the moat south to **Sakurada Gate** (Sakurada-mon). Dating from 1620, it's the largest existing gate of Tokyo Castle. Although damaged by the Great Kanto Earthquake of 1923, the gate was rebuilt and is designated an 'Important Cultural Asset'.

Tokyo (Edo) Castle, Chiyoda-ku; Tue–Thur and Sat–Sun 9am–4.30pm; free; map D4

Visit Yasukuni-jinja, controversial shrine to Japan's war dead

You might have seen it in the news; now tour the shrine that troubles relations between Japan and its Korean and Chinese neighbours. On entering **Yasukuni-jinja** via its towering *torii* (shrine gate), you'd never suspect that such tranquil grounds could be the flashpoint for disputes over wartime history between these East Asian giants. Towering gingko trees, a staple of shrines across Japan, line the approach to the stately building.

Memorialised at Yasukuni are the souls of some 2.5 million soldiers who have died in wars fought since its completion in 1869. Among them are the First Sino-Japanese War, the Russo-Japanese War, the Second Sino-Japanese War and World War II. Behind the shrine lies a quaint **teahouse** and **sumo ring** where bouts are held during the spring festival.

Emperor Hirohito stopped visiting Yasukuni from 1978 until his death in 1989, reportedly because it enshrined notorious war criminals. Recent annual visits by Japanese politicians have generated blowback from China and the Koreas, who contend that the shrine glorifies Japan's 20th-century military aggression.

But it's the on-site **Yushukan War Museum**, with its self-justifying interpretation of history (war dead are referred to as 'divinities'), that offers the most intriguing aspect of a visit. Plaques that accompany objects such as a human suicide torpedo consistently paint World War II as an inevitability that Japan did its best to avoid, glossing over the atrocities committed by the Imperial forces.

Yasukuni-jinja; 3-1-1 Kudankita, Chiyoda-ku; tel: 3261-8326; www.yasukuni.or.jp; map C5
Yushukan War Museum; address and map as above; www.yasukuni.or.jp/english/yushukan; daily 9am–4.30pm; charge

Grasp how Japan's artists responded to Western modernity at the National Museum of Modern Art, Tokyo

The **National Museum of Modern Art, Tokyo (MOMAT)** has its share of Chagalls and Picassos, but you didn't travel thousands of miles to see second-rate pieces by Western artists. What makes MOMAT important is its outstanding collection of art by 20th-century Japanese artists. Taken as a whole, they tell the story of how figures like Ryusei Kishida and Taikan Yokoyama took up the challenge posed by the Modernist revolution. Deeply influenced by European movements such as Impressionism, Japan's artists turned these techniques to local subject matter, and attempted valiantly to synthesise traditional approaches with the new forces filtering in from the West.

Designed by architect Yoshiro Taniguchi and completed in 1969, MOMAT sits amid peaceful grounds just north of the Imperial Palace. In galleries on the second to fourth floors, 'MOMAT Collection' presents 200 important works selected from more than 12,000 items. Exhibits range from Japanese- and Western-style paintings to prints and sculptures, photographs and videos, which trace Japan's artistic history from the beginning of the 20th century to the present day.

If you still have the energy, don't miss the nearby **Crafts Gallery**, which displays superb ceramics, wood and other treasures in a century-old red-brick building that once housed the Imperial Guard. Just across the road is the Chidorigafuchi pond, a lovely spot for viewing cherry blossoms in spring.

National Museum of Modern Art, Tokyo (MOMAT; Kokuritsu Kindai Bijutsukan); 3-1 Kitanomarukoen, Chiyoda-ku; tel: 5777-8600; www.momat.go.jp; Tue–Thu and Sun 10am–5pm, Fri–Sat until 8pm; charge; map D5
Crafts Gallery; 1-1 Kitanomarukoen; Chiyoda-ku, Tue–Sun 10am–5pm; charge; map D5

Take in a performance of exotic *Kabuki* at the newly refurbished Kabuki-za

Tourists may well perceive *Kabuki* to be the ultimate in refined Japanese high culture. Nothing could be further from the reality. While *Kabuki* is indeed a national treasure, the theatre form began in the 1600s as subversive, ribald sketches frequently portrayed by prostitutes – until the shoguns banned it. When it was revived, male actors began to play the female roles, resulting in the *onnagata* (female part) technique for which *Kabuki* is justly famous.

These days, *Kabuki* is performed at Ginza's **Kabuki-za theatre**. The building reopened in 2013 following a three-year renovation with the controversial addition of a soaring glass tower affixed to the back.

Those wishing to indulge in this exotic, stylised art form are advised to sample a tourist-friendly one-act performance for the wallet-friendly price of ¥1200.

To an extent, what you get is what you pay for. You will be directed to the fourth floor, high above the stage, which doesn't offer the best views but still allows clear sightlines to the actors below. An English audio guide is highly advisable if one hopes to make any sense of *Kabuki*'s plotlines, often a dizzying series of events that, delivered in archaic Japanese, is sonically piquant if incomprehensible.

Kabuki-za theatre; 4-12-15 Ginza, Chuo-ku; tel: 3545-6800; www.kabuki-bito.jp/eng; map F2

Dine at swanky Marubiru as you gaze over scintillating Tokyo Station

Towering in front of the Marunouchi exit of Tokyo Station, the **Marunouchi Building** – Marubiru to locals – was one of the first mixed-use office-

Tokyo Station

Completed in 1914 in front of the Palace Garden, **Tokyo Station** (www.tokyostationcity.com/en) symbolised the aspirations of pre-war Imperial Japan. Over a century of history, the grand structure has witnessed the assassination of two prime ministers. It suffered extensive damage in World War II, after which the original domes were replaced with angled roofs. Today, the station gleams from an extensive renovation (completed in 2012). It's Japan's busiest in terms of trains per day, with more than a dozen commuter lines as well as the subway, and of course the high-speed Shinkansen bullet train accessing all parts of the country. If that isn't enough, there's a hotel, a museum and shops and restaurants a plenty.

retail skyscrapers to pop up in the now glittering Tokyo Station area.

The impressive building, which in 2002 replaced a 1923 structure that was once Asia's tallest, has excellent dining options and incomparable views of the refurbished **Tokyo Station** – best enjoyed at night when the station is impressively illuminated.

Any east-facing restaurant will offer good views of the stately edifice, but aim for the stylish, delectable **Casablanca Silk**, which serves delicious Vietnamese cuisine.

The fifth floor offers a range of tasty non-Japanese offerings, but if you're hankering for local flavours head to the sixth floor for everything from *kaiseki* (multi-course) cuisine to *okonomiyaki* (savoury pancakes).

Casablanca Silk; 2-4-1 Marunouchi, Chiyoda-ku, Tokyo Marunouchi Bldg. 5F; tel: 5220-5612; Mon–Sat 11am–11pm, Sun until 10pm; map E3/4

Shop at the world's fanciest stores on Ginza's premium Chuo-dori

Ginza means 'silver mint' and takes its name from a mint established by the Shogun Tokugawa Ieyasu in 1612. For centuries, the area east of the Imperial Palace has been Japan's premier destination for luxury goods. While in recent years discount shops have opened to cater to cash-poor youths and Chinese tourists on shopping binges, the main Chuo-dori drag has countered with a series of contemporary complexes hosting the chicest of boutiques.

For some extremely classy one-stop shopping, make for Ginza's historic department stores. Occupying what is said to be Japan's most prestigious address at Ginza 4-chome, the well-heeled **Wako Honkan** (4-5-11 Ginza, Chuo-ku; tel: 3562-2111; www.wako.co.jp/en; map E/F2) is housed in one of only a few buildings to have survived the World War II firebombings. Inside you'll find watches (the shop is owned by Seiko), jewellery, men and women's goods and interior decor, often specially developed based on feedback from Japan's wealthiest consumers.

Directly across the street is Mitsukoshi's Ginza outpost. Founded in 1673, **Mitsukoshi** (4-6-16, Ginza, Chuo-ku; tel: 3562-1111; www.mitsukoshi.co.jp; map F2) takes pride of place as the most venerable department store chain in Japan. The Ginza version pales in comparison to the hulking Nihon-bashi main store, but nevertheless offers a refined selection of mainly women's clothes.

Diagonally opposite Wako is the brand-new **Ginza Place** (5-8-1 Ginza, Chuo-ku; ginzaplace.jp; map E2), a striking architectural confection designed by Klein Dytham Architects and opened in 2016. Inside, you'll find **Nissan** and **Sony**'s new global flagship showrooms and five restaurants and cafés, including Parisian celebrity chef Thierry Marx's **Bistro Marx**.

Ginza also houses numerous outposts of luxury Western brands like Chanel, Tiffany and Gucci, along with an Apple Store. But for local flavour, head to **Mikimoto** (2-4-12 Ginza, Chuo-ku; tel: 3535-4611; www.mikimoto.com/en/index.html; map F2), whose founder Kokichi Mikimoto created the world's first cultured pearl. For more than a century Japan's high society has relied on Mikimoto for the finest quality pearl jewellery.

Japan is justly famous for its exactly crafted pens and pencils, as well as its artistic, handmade *washi* paper. This makes a visit to the Itoya stationery chain's Ginza flagship a joyful occasion. **G. Itoya** (as it's been called since its 2015 revamp) boasts a lovely display of stationery – you can even pen and post a card to friends back home from the shop's second-floor SHARE Space (Ginza 2-7-15, Chuo-ku; tel: 3561-8311; www.ito-ya.co.jp; map F2).

If the kids are in tow, head to another Ginza standby, **Haku-hinkan Toy Park** (8-8-11 Ginza, Chuo-ku; tel: 3571-8008; www.hakuhinkan.co.jp; map E2). From Tomica toy cars to Nintendo game devices to Licca-chan dolls (the Japanese Barbie), the shop packs all that is finely made and/or wacky about Japanese toys into its four floors of shopping, with an extra two floors of restaurants and theatre to top it off.

Much Western culture was introduced to Japan first in Ginza, which makes a meal at **Shiseido Parlour** (8-8-3 Ginza, Chuo-ku; http://parlour.shiseido.co.jp/en/index.html; map E2) a suitable and educational way to round off your retail-therapy experience. An innovator of the Japanese take on Western cuisine known as *yoshoku*, the restaurant has been serving dishes like croquettes (deep-fried veg or meat patties pronounced 'ko-ro-keh') and *omuraisu* (omelettes stuffed with seasoned rice) since 1902. A third-floor café whips up tasty interpretations of fruit parfaits and ice-cream sodas, befitting its status as the first establishment to sell soda in the country.

Catch a kitschy drag musical by the venerable Takarazuka Revue

If the men playing women of traditional *Kabuki* theatre aren't your thing, how about women playing men? That's the promise of the **Takarazuka Revue** – along with a heady dose of glitter, razzle-dazzle, song and dance.

Created by the president of Hankyu Railways in 1913 to draw tourists to the westerly town of Takarazuka, the Revue exploded after a ground-breaking production of *Rose of Versailles*, the famous shoujo (girls) manga. Today, the company has the Grand Theater in Takarazuka and the **Tokyo Takarazuka Theater**, welcoming millions of star-struck fans every year.

Thousands of young women audition annually to join the Revue, but only a talented 50 or so are chosen. The lucky victors join one of five companies with names like Moon Troupe and Snow Troupe, depending on their specific strengths.

While its fame took off with an adaption of the *Rose of Versailles*, contemporary productions often take the lead from West End and Broadway. Recent shows have included adaptions of *The Scarlet Pimpernel* and *Grand Hotel*, with even kitschier offerings in the form of a woman playing the romantic lead samurai in a drama set in ancient Japan called *Wind Over Yamatai-koku*.

Tickets go quickly, so it is best to book before your trip. The theatre will be packed with a fervent audience; after a performance there is often a rousing encore that gets people out of their seats, belting out their beloved favourites.

Tokyo Takarazuka Theater; 1-1-3 Yurakucho, Chiyoda-ku; tel: 5251-2001; map E2

Sip tea at a beautifully serene traditional garden

After the hustle and bustle of Ginza, escape to the quiet of **Hamarikyu**, just south and east of the shopping district. Located at the mouth of the Sumida River, it was once the site of a Shogun Tokugawa family villa in the 17th century.

Opened as a public garden in 1946, Hamarikyu now serves as an urban oasis made all the more important by the inaccessibility of the Imperial Palace, and its status as one of the largest areas of greenery in central Tokyo

Built on reclaimed land around a tidal pond, Hamarikyu's gardens were planted by successive shoguns in a style typical of the Edo Era. Black pines are interspersed with camellia and apricot trees, along with the traditional flowering Sakura cherry trees, around which the Japanese gather in spring for hanami (blossom-viewing parties).

A stone bridge leads across the pond to the **teahouse**, a trip to which is the highlight of a visit to Hamarikyu. While authentic *sado* (tea ceremonies) call for the pricey services of a *sensei*, the Hamarikyu teahouse offers a self-guided tea ceremony.

For a reasonable ¥510, visitors are provided with a cup of green (*matcha*) tea and a sweet, called a *wagashi*, which has an important meaning in a Japanese tea ceremony. An instruction sheet explains the order in which to accomplish the simple but elegant ritual, as well as the proper way to hold your bowl and eat your confection.

Hamarikyu; 1-1, Hama Rikyu-teien, Chuo-ku; tel: 3541-0200; http://teien.tokyo-park.or.jp/en/hama-rikyu; daily 9am–5pm; map E1

Indulge in haute cuisine at the plush Conrad hotel

The Peninsula, The Ritz-Carlton, The Mandarin Oriental... after a luxury hotel building boom they're all here now. But none in the central district can better the unparalleled mix of indulgence and views of the **Conrad Tokyo**. The hotel occupies the top 10 floors of the 37-storey Tokyo Shiodome Building, granting gorgeous views of the Hamarikyu Gardens and the bayside skyline.

If you're not staying at the Conrad, you can still revel in its extravagance. Topping the list is a meal at the **Collage** French restaurant on the 28th floor. The establishment is helmed by Kyoto-born chef, Shinya Maeda, who studied under the legendary Gordon Ramsay.

Maeda takes an eccentric approach to French cuisine, having worked at some of London's top dining establishments before heading to New York's famed Aquavit. In 2008, when Maeda was only 34 years old, he was handpicked by Ramsay to head the kitchen of his restaurant at the Conrad, where he earned a Michelin star in his very first year. In 2013, the restaurant reopened as Collage with Maeda as Chef de Cuisine.

Maeda's international background is reflected in his menu: an amuse bouche of fois gras could be followed by a Vietnamese spring roll or a dish taken from Japanese *kaiseki* (multi-course) cuisine, and rounded off with a dessert soufflé. All of it will be scrumptious, seasonal and accompanied by the choicest wines.

Conrad Tokyo; 1-9-1 Higashi-Shinbashi, Minato-ku; tel: 6388-8000; www.conrad tokyo.co.jp; Collage Tue–Sat noon–9pm, Sun until 2pm; map E1

Rub shoulders with after-work salarymen at Shimbashi's Yakitori Alley

Tokyo has received a lot of press as the world's capital of Michelin-starred cuisine. But for a taste of how Japan's salt of the earth really eat, head for Shimbashi's **'Yakitori Alley'** (map E2).

Tucked into an underpass beneath the famed bullet train tracks is a warren of tiny *izakaya* (drinking and dining establishments) and food stalls serving *yakitori* (grilled chicken skewers). Legions of salarymen head here to dine, enjoy a brew, smoke and to blow off steam after another tiring day at the office.

Yakitori Alley is best reached from Hibiya Station. Surface at exit A2, turn right where the stairs reach the road and walk straight alongside the tracks until you glimpse the neon lights and detect the unmistakable scent of a thousand chicken skewers grilling.

Some of the shops have taken on a permanent aspect, and the success of Yakitori Alley means it has now expanded into the adjacent block. But the crowded nest of shops – stools spilling onto the streets – is one of the few reminders of the ramshackle, improvised Tokyo of the post-war era.

Now it's time to take your pick of the stalls – any will do – and

come to grips with the menu. *Yakitori* doesn't mean only the easily digestible white meat we've come to depend on in the west. In Shimbashi, expect to choose from heart, intestines, gizzards... even uterus! A skewer costs ¥1–200, and for the faint of heart there's white meat, *tsukune* (chicken balls) and even veggie options. Take your pick between *shio* (salt) and *tare* (sweetened soy sauce), and wash it all down with a Sapporo or Asahi.

Eat succulent sushi and browse the bustling Tsukiji Outer Market

At the time of writing, the move of the world's biggest wholesale fish market (formally the **Tokyo Central Wholesale Market**) from Tsukiji to a new location was embroiled in controversy over toxic waste found in soil beneath the new Toyosu location.

But this is of concern only to the hardy few who wake in darkness to observe the tuna auctions themselves. Most people don't bother and simply experience the bustling **Tsukiji Outer Market**, which thankfully is staying put.

More than 2,000 tonnes of fish move through Tsukiji each day. A portion of that – and the freshest of all due to its location adjacent to **Inner Market** – winds up in the tiny eateries that pack the ramshackle buildings known as the Outer Market.

From Tsukiji Station, head southwest on Shin-Ohashi-dori past Tsukiji

Hongan-ji, an imposing temple. On the far side of the Harumi-dori intersection you'll soon find, on the left, all manner of shops hawking everything from traditional Japanese kitchenware and food wholesalers to crafts and even taxidermy products. These are worth a visit in themselves, but head to the market first.

Continue on and turn left just before the large, ugly concrete structure that is the wholesale market. You'll find yourself in a warren of delightful sushi shops and other eateries that make up the Outer Market. The market's popularity means they tend to be crowded, but they're equipped with English menus and are comfortable serving foreigners. No need to be fussy – the fish is equally fresh anywhere. A sushi set will set you back ¥2–3000. Make sure to get there before 2pm when business winds down for the day.

Tsukiji Market; 4-16-2 Tsukiji, Chuo-ku; www.tsukiji-market.or.jp; map F1

The Outer Market

The Outer Market is a superb area to browse unique souvenirs for friends and family back home. A detailed English Tsukiji Guide Map is available for download from the Outer Market website.

Gallery hop Tokyo's densest concentration of art galleries

The backstreets of Ginza provide a welcome contrast to brash Chuo-dori. Where the main drag is relentless in its devotion to commerce, the narrower streets on either side temper retail galore with art and nightlife. If you're big on art, *Tokyo Art Beat* (www.tokyoartbeat.com) is a useful resource, with updated exhibition listings and pointed reviews.

Start your tour of Tokyo's densest concentration of art galleries at Shiseido Parlour (see page 35). The basement of this building, run by the cosmetics giant Shiseido, houses the **Shiseido Gallery**, in operation since 1919 and said to be the oldest continuous gallery in Japan. In the 1990s, the gallery shifted its emphasis to contemporary art; it has played a role in fostering the careers of numerous young artists such as photographer Rinko Kawauchi and manga-influenced video-artist Tabaimo.

Also not to be missed is **Gallery Koyanagi**. One of Tokyo's most prestigious spaces, Koyanagi represents artists who have gone on to international fame including Makoto Aida, Akira Yamaguchi and (like the Shiseido Gallery) Tabaimo.

For a change from fine art, the **Ginza Graphic Gallery**, run by printing giant Dai Nippon, presents graphic designs by major Japanese and international creators.

The Okuno Building offers a pleasing break from corporate-run galleries. A 1930s apartment building, it houses a number of tiny art spaces featuring the work of mostly young artists. Check into Room 306, where the **Ginza Okuno Building Room-306 Project** non-profit runs a series of rotating shows.

Shiseido Gallery; 8-8-3 Ginza Chuo-ku; tel: 3572-3901; www.shiseidogroup.com/gallery/index.html; weekdays 11am–7pm, Sun until 6pm; map E2

Gallery Koyanagi; 9F, 1-7-5 Ginza Chuo-ku; tel: 3561-1896; www.gallerykoyanagi.com; Tue–Sat 11am–7pm; map E2

Ginza Graphic Gallery; 7-7-2 Ginza, Chuo-ku; tel: 3571-5206; www.dnp.co.jp/gallery/ggg_e; Mon–Sat 11am–7pm; map E2

Ginza Okuno Building Room-306 Project; 1-9-8 Ginza, Chuo-ku; http://306project.web.fc2.com/eg-home.htm; hours vary; map E2

Hark back to the 1930s and sip a cup of flannel-brewed coffee at Tricolore Honten

Coffee came late to Japan, but the Japanese didn't waste any time making it their own. Despite their name, *kissaten* ('tea drinking rooms') are a unique form of Japanese coffee shop, many of which specialise in unique brewing methods and encourage customers to linger to listen to jazz and classical music. Despite encroachments by Starbucks and its domestic rivals, the most venerable of the lot – places like Ginza's **Tricolore Honten** – are bucking the trend with aplomb.

Enter Tricolore and step back to the 1930s ('36 to be precise), a time when Ginza was the place to see and be seen as people tested out the new Western ways. Everything from the ivy-draped exterior to the bone china, to the silver and chandeliers, says we take our coffee seriously. Each cup is made from top-quality coffee beans from Central and South America, which are brewed and then dripped into each coffee through a special cotton flannel filter. The cloth filters are said to allow for an incredibly clean cup with excellent filtration, without the papery tastes that come from paper filters.

The morning egg breakfast set is delicious, with extra-thick toast and salad, and Tricolore is also renowned for its stunning baked goods – the cheesecake in particular gets rave reviews.

Tricolore Honten; 5-9-17 Ginza, Chuo-ku; tel: 3571-1811; www.tricolore.co.jp; 8am–9pm; map F2

Locate the secret trap door and dine at Ninja Restaurant

Japan seems to be experiencing something of a ninja boom of late. Ninja schools and ninja events are popping up like surprise assassins in the night. These medieval warriors, skilled in the arts of stealth and shock, provide the concept for one of Tokyo's liveliest themed restaurants. Yes, there's a ninja restaurant in New York. But would it be as fun as visiting **Ninja Restaurant** in the land of the ninja?

You enter via a slot door and find yourself in a darkened vestibule. A ninja then appears to escort you through a secret passageway (complete with a drawbridge) into a dark dungeon of a restaurant. Ninjas glide to and fro as you look at your menu. Themed restaurants can let themselves down when it comes to the actual food, but Ninja Restaurant makes a pretty serious effort, with mostly successful results.

But the cuisine comes with a chunky price tag. The cheapest tasting-course menu costs ¥5,700, and begins with crunchy Shuriken star-blades grissini, followed by chicken fritter (ninja style) and a special stone-boiled soup, a seafood special of the day and dessert. The top-of-the-line Jyubei menu will set you back ¥15,000, but includes lobster, deluxe Japa-

nese wagyu beef steak with cedar fragrance and a 'Snow crab and grapefruit served with a sword trick'. Should you forgo a course, a la carte items can be ordered for ¥600 for an appetiser up to ¥4,500 for a simple steak. Reservations are required.

Ninja Restaurant; 2-14-3 Nagatacho, Chiyoda ku; tel: 5157-3936; http://ninja akasaka.com; Mon–Sat 5pm–1am, Sun until 11.30pm; map B3

Master the essentials of sushi preparation

Yes, it takes 10 years to become a proper Japanese sushi chef, but you can learn a lot in 90 minutes. That's the essence of a starter sushi workshop offered by the **Tokyo Sushi Academy** in Tsukiji, the font of all things fishy in the capital.

Sidle up to a table under the guidance of one of the Academy's chef-instructors. Many have worked overseas and are fluent in English. Your chef will patiently guide you through the correct steps for shaping rice, and placing fish perfectly in position in its perch atop. Then you'll be taught what the school calls the 'sushi move', which provides just the right amount of pressure to form an ideal union of rice and fish in the local style called *Edo-mae*.

You can choose from one of about eight types of fish or egg, and also get the chance to dress up in a sushi costume for selfies to post on social media. And, of course, you get to eat the sushi once you're done. Kid's courses are available.

If you're ready to branch out beyond sushi, **Tsukiji Cooking** offers classes in the delicate art of fluffy tempura frying, braising with teriyaki sauce and even making a type of Japanese sweet called *daifuku mochi*, consisting of *mochi* (rice gluten) stuffed with sweet red-bean paste and a strawberry.

Tokyo Sushi Academy; 4-7-5 Tsukiji, Chuo-ku; tel: 6264-7858; http://sushimaking. tokyo; map F2
Tsukiji Cooking; 6-22-3 Tsukiji, Chuo-ku; tel: 5966-4378; http://tsukiji-cooking.com; map F1

Experience the art of Japan's geisha up close and personal

First, let's dispense with the myth that geisha are high-class courtesans. They are trained entertainers who spend years mastering traditional performing arts and conversation methods. While an evening spent being entertained by geisha at a posh restaurant could set you back a small fortune, it's now easy to get a glimpse into the world of geisha for an hour and not end up in the poorhouse.

This is made possible by **Omotenashi Nihonbashi**, a programme of Japanese cultural experiences organised by the Nihonbashi Information Center. A large *tatami* (woven straw) mat and tearoom inside **Coredo Muromachi Shopping Center** in Nihonbashi accommodate the sessions.

The starter, one-hour programme is called 'Time To Geisha'. Enter and be mesmerised as geisha dance and sing to the intriguing sound of the *shamisen* (a kind of Japanese banjo). Participants then play interactive games that have been passed on for centuries; women will be fitted with a beautiful kimono to make the experience even more memorable.

Omotenashi Nihonbashi offers several other cultural experiences, ranging from tea ceremonies to *washi* (traditional handmade paper) cutting and origami paper folding.

Omotenashi Nihonbashi; 2-2-1 Nihonbashi Muromachi, Chuo-ku; tel: 3242-2334; www.nihonbashi-info.jp/omotenashi/index. html; daily 10am–9pm; map G4

ROPPONGI AND AKASAKA

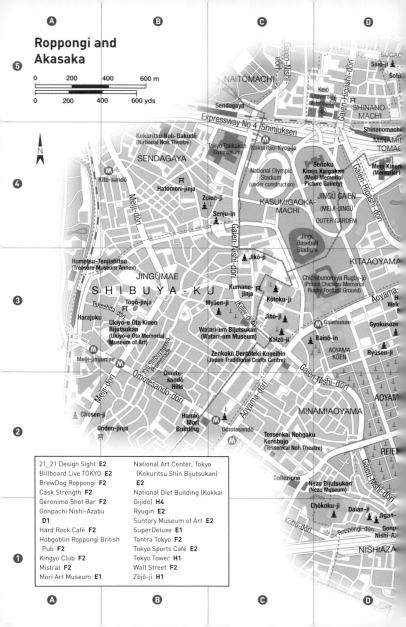

Roppongi and Akasaka

Scale:
0 — 200 — 400 — 600 m
0 — 200 — 400 — 600 yds

NAITOMACHI
SUGAC
Saio-ji
Sotu
Keiō University & Hospital
SHINANO-MACHI
Sendagaya
Expressway No 4 Shinjuksen
MINAMI-TOMAC
Shinanomachi
Kokuritsu Noh-Gakudō (National Noh Theatre)
Tokyo Taiikukan (Gymnasium)
Kokuritsu-Kyogijo
SENDAGAYA
Meiji Kinen (Memorial F)
National Olympic Stadium (under construction)
Seitoku Kinen Kaigakan (Meiji Memorial Picture Gallery)
Kita-sandō
Meiji-dōri
Hatomori-jinja
Zūlen-ji
KASUMIGAOKA-MACHI
JINGŪ GAIEN (MEIJI-JINGŪ) OUTER GARDEN)
Senju-in
Homotsu-Tenjishitsu (Treasure Museum Annex)
Jikō-ji
Jingū Baseball Stadium
KITAAOYAMA
JINGŪMAE
Kumano-jinja
Chichibunomiya Rugby-jo (Prince Chichibu Memorial Rugby Football Ground)
S H I B U Y A - K U
Takeshita-dōri
Tōgō-jinja
Myōen-ji
Kōtoku-ji
Aoyama
We
Harajuku
Ukiyo-e Ōta Kinen Bijutsukan (Ukiyo-e Ōta Memorial Museum of Art)
Watari-um Bijutsukan (Watari-um Museum)
Jihō-ji
Gaienmae
Gyokusōze
Meiji-jingūmae
Kaizō-ji
Baisō-in
AOYAMA KŌEN
Ryūsen-ji
Zenkoku Dentōteki Kogeihin (Japan Traditional Crafts Centre)
Omote-sandō Hills
Omotesandō-dōri
Gaien-Nishi-dōri
AOYAM
Chōsen-ji
MINAMIAOYAMA
Onden-jinja
Hanae Mori Building
Omotesandō
Tessenkai Nohgaku Kenshujo (Tessenkai Noh Theatre)
REIE
Collezione
Nezu Bijutsukan (Nezu Museum)
Chōkoku-ji
Daian-ji
Jigan-
Kottō-dōri
Roppongi-dōri
Gonp Nishi-A
NISHIAZA

Contemplate cutting-edge art at the Mori Art Museum high above Roppongi Hills

The Mori Art Museum (MAM) bills itself as 'Japan's leading contemporary art museum', and despite some competition from the Museum of Contemporary Art, Tokyo (MOT), the Hara and Watari-um, it generally lives up to its boast. The capacious museum is located at the top of the Roppongi Hills Mori Tower skyscraper in the Roppongi entertainment district. At its helm are far-sighted director Fumio Nanjo and ambitious chief curator Mami Kataoka.

Developer Minoru Mori crowned his imposing tower with a museum in the belief that, 'culture shapes a city's identity'. Under Nanjo and Kataoka's guidance, the Mori has done just that.

The Mori hosts visionary exhibitions, primarily of Japanese and Asian art. Kataoka has curated a number of influential shows, including 'Ai Weiwei: According to What?' in 2009, which toured the

> **Roppongi Art Triangle**
> The other two corners of the 'Roppongi Art Triangle' are the **National Art Center Tokyo (NACT)** and **21_21 Design Sight**.

United States, and diverse exhibitions such as the regular 'Roppongi Crossing', in which her deep knowledge of art trends is evident.

The Mori has also shaped Tokyo's art scene by making itself a locus of events such as the annual Tokyo Art Night, now one of the major art events in Tokyo with nearly a million people burning the midnight oil in order to view art installations and performances in 2016.

The Mori is reached by a futuristic elevator that deposits you on the 53rd floor lobby. After imbibing the art, head down a floor to the Tokyo City View observation deck for panoramic vistas of central Tokyo, best experienced at sunset. Recharge with a coffee or meal at **The Sun & The Moon** museum café and restaurant.

Mori Art Museum (bijutsukan); 6-10-1 Roppongi, Minato-ku; museum Wed–Mon 10am–10pm, Tue until 5pm, The Sun & The Moon daily 11am–11pm; tel: 5777-8600; www.mori.art.museum; charge; map E1

Catch a jazz show with a cityscape backdrop at Billboard Live TOKYO

Tokyo has three swish supper clubs, but for sheer impressiveness, **Billboard Live TOKYO** takes the crown.

The club operates out of a fourth-floor space in the Midtown building, overlooking the garden next to the complex. The high-ceilinged venue is backed by a vast window that sets off performers against the Tokyo night skyline. A more dramatic backdrop is hard to come by.

The 300-capacity Billboard Live TOKYO is operated as a franchise by Hanshin Contents Link, a curious subsidiary of Osaka-based Hanshin Electric Railway Co. Befit-

ting the music-industry magazine from where it gets its name, the club opened in 2006 with jazz-rock giants Steely Dan.

Billboard Live TOKYO and its Osaka sister continue to attract big-league talent. Recent listings include Belinda Carlisle, Ray Parker Jr. and Joe, along with top-ranked J-pop singers like Crystal Kay and Chu Kosaka.

Get your credit card ready and prepare to pop the bubbly as you relax in velvet chairs, groove to the tunes and absorb the view.

Billboard Live TOKYO; Midtown Garden Terrace, 7-4-9-4F Akasaka, Minato-ku; tel: 3405-1133; www.billboard-live.com; map E2

Alternative supper clubs

As befits the world's biggest metropolis, Tokyo boasts two more fancy supper clubs. **Blue Note Tokyo** (6-3-16 Minami-Aoyama, Minato-ku; tel: 5485-0088; http://bluenote. co.jp) is the veteran, and for die-hard jazz fans, still the place to be. Its plush basement space hosts artists like Pat Metheny and Chick Corea. Also offering a luxurious dinner, drinks and music experience is **Marunouchi's Cotton Club** (2-7-3 Marunouchi, Chiyoda-ku; tel: 3215-1555; www.cottonclubjapan.co.jp), where bookings tend to be slightly more progressive.

Be entertained at the foot of Tokyo Tower before ascending for the views

Completed in 1958, **Tokyo Tower** was for decades Japan's tallest structure, and a symbol of the nation's post-war rebirth. It was eclipsed in 2012 by the opening of Tokyo Skytree (see page 144), but the Tower's location makes for superior views of the city centre. Tokyo Tower is also still the world's highest self-supported steel tower. It's been destroyed in countless *kaiju* monster films and climbed by King Kong, making it an icon the world over. The truly bold can climb it via a vertiginous 600-step staircase.

At 492 and 820ft (150 and 250 metres), the viewing platforms have been outdone by Skytree's, but they still offer stellar perspectives of the capital, best enjoyed at night. The lower deck offers a thrilling, glass-floored Lookdown Window. The higher observatory will reopen in summer 2017 after undergoing an extensive renovation.

Approached from the base, the tower is a more prosaic structure. A five-storey mall called Foot Town houses a number of entertainment enterprises, including a middling aquarium and a new mini theme park, **Tokyo One Piece Tower,** opened in 2015 and based on the popular manga series *One Piece*. Written by Eiichiro Oda, the series follows the adventures of young Monkey D. Luffy and his crew of pirates as they search for the 'One Piece' treasure, necessary to become the next King of the Pirates. Fans of the franchise can enjoy carnival games, watch a live action show that uses projection mapping or dine on – you guessed it – *One Piece* food.

Others may want to pass on the theme park and instead munch some 'B-grade' cuisine – a Japanese term for food that bucks 'quality' mainstream trends in favour of keeping a distinct identity. Try the shop serving *taiyaki*, a kind of Japanese cake most often filled with sweet-bean paste or custard.

Tokyo Tower; 4-2-8 Shibakoen, Minato-ku; www.tokyotower.co.jp; daily 9am–11pm; map H1
Tokyo One Piece Tower; address and map as above; https://onepiecetower. tokyo/?lang=en; daily 10am–10pm

Tour stately Zojo-ji, the temple where six Tokugawa shoguns are entombed

Standing next to Tokyo Tower, **Zojo-ji** is one of Tokyo's most impressive temples, and the centre of the Jodo sect of Buddhism in the capital area. A visit to its serene precinct offers a noble counterpoint to Tokyo Tower's crude commercialism.

Founded in 1393 as a seminary, Zojo-ji acquired new importance when the first shogun, Ieyasu Tokugawa, established his rule over Edo (present-day Tokyo) in 1590. It became the Tokugawa family temple, and was upgraded as a show of their immense wealth and power. In total, six of the 15 Tokugawa shoguns are buried at Zojo-ji.

The **main hall** (Hondo) that you see today dates only from 1974, but several structures on the grounds are national treasures. First and foremost is the magnificent **main gate** (Sangedatsu-mon).

Constructed in 1622, the vermilion-lacquered gate is one of the few reminders of the Shoguns' unrivalled prosperity to have survived Tokyo's quakes and bombings, and is a designated 'Important Cultural Property'. Gaze up at all 69ft (21 metres) of it, and see images of Shakyamuni Buddha, Samantabhadra and Manjusri bodhisattvas, created by Kyoto's Buddhist sculptors when Zojo-ji was built.

Also of note is the **Bill Bell** (Dai-bonsho). Dating from 1673, the bell stands 10.8ft (3.3 metres) tall and weighs more than 13 tonnes. It's renowned as one of the Big Three Bells of the Edo Period.

Before you depart, spend a solemn moment contemplating the **Unborn Children Garden**. Rows of stone statues of children represent unborn babies, including the miscarried, aborted and stillborn. These are a common feature of Japan's temples. Parents often decorate them with clothing and toys, offering gifts for Jizo, the guardian of unborn children, to ensure their passage to the afterlife.

Zojo-ji; 4-7-35 Shiba-Koen, Minato-ku; tel: 3423-1431; www.zojoji.or.jp; map H1

Get a taste of Japanese politics at the impressive National Diet Building

The Imperial Palace may be the heart of Japanese tradition, but the **National Diet Building** is the locus of the nation's power. The grand, 1936 construction houses the two main branches of government: the House of Councillors and House of Representatives. Debates appear regularly on Japanese TV and important meetings are often screened live. Tours are not only free, but are unexpectedly fascinating, even to the uninformed.

The current National Diet Building was the result of a lengthy design and building process. After the first and second Diet buildings burnt down, a commission chose a design by Fukuzo Watanabe that fused Asian and Western elements.

Both houses offer free tours. Tours of the House of Councillors happen every hour from 9am to 4pm on weekdays. Visitors simply show up at the west entry of the Diet, fill out a short visitor's form, do a quick security check and proceed on the tour. You will be shown the public gallery of the main chamber, the Imperial family's waiting rooms, the Central Hall and the garden in the main courtyard. Tours are in Japanese but an English pamphlet is provided.

Of more interest is the tour of the (more powerful) House of Representatives, which must be reserved 10 days in advance. It is conducted in English on Monday and Thursday afternoons. The tour follows a similar pattern to that of the House of Councillors tour, but offers far more insight into the legislative process.

National Diet Building (Kokkai-gijido); 1-7-1 Nagatacho, Chiyoda-ku; tel: 5521-7445; www.sangiin.go.jp; map H4

Diet Library cafeteria
After you've worked up an appetite, dine elbow-to-elbow with politicians and bureaucrats at the Diet Library cafeteria, just one block north of the Diet Building.

Experience a transsexual cabaret show – and then drink with the cast – at Kingyo Club

Get ready for something truly risqué.

Kingyo Club represents a new iteration of a long Japanese history of gender-bending theatrics. In the '90s, the cabaret here sprung out of a tradition of show pubs, but with a twist. Where show pubs often feature beautiful, young women of limited talent, the shows at Kingyo Club are largely performed by skilled 'new half' or transsexual actors in various stages of transition from male to female.

This doesn't seem odd in Japan, where TV variety shows often feature highly successful transsexual entertainers, and where homosexual relationships were widely recognised among the samurai classes. The upshot is that while LGBTQ culture is still in its infancy as a *political* movement, Japan has long had a flexible attitude towards gender and its fluidity.

Enter Kingyo Club and you will be ushered into a small but well-equipped theatre, served dinner and drinks, and treated to a series of song-and-dance skits. The concept is 'neo-*Kabuki*' and the staging is flashy, but the topics can be highly politicised, for example critiquing the US base presence in Japan.

What Kingyo Club shares with other show pubs in Japan is

this: after the show is done, cast members will emerge from the greenroom and ply you with drinks while they chat you up at your table. Expect to pay roughly ¥7,000 for the show, drinks and dinner.

Kingyo Club; 3-14-17 Roppongi, Minato-ku; tel: 3478-3000; http://kingyo.co.jp; shows at 7.30 and 10pm, closed Mon; map F2

Sip rarefied Japanese whisky at underground hideaway Cask Strength

It's no secret now that Japan produces some of the world's finest whiskies. And few bars in Tokyo have as rich a selection, or as inviting an atmosphere in which to drink it, as **Cask Strength**.

Entering through the stone entrance and descending down a passageway, it feels like you've arrived at a medieval Scottish manor. Once inside you'll be greeted by dignified, bow-tied bartenders working their magic behind a dark, wooden bar backed by towering ranks of alcohol – many of them the finest whiskies the world has to offer.

Like many high-end bars in Japan, Cask Strength requires customers pay a ¥1,000 table charge. For this you will receive a small beer snack, which on any given night could be a small arrangement of Japanese crackers or deep-fried soba noodles.

There's a bewildering array of top-flight spirits to choose from. Should you wish, say, to order a 1968 Bowmore Scotch, it's possible, but beware that it could cost you anything up to around US$150! It is usually best to ask the bartender to write the price of your order beforehand.

Anyway, you didn't come all this way to drink Scotch whisky. Cask Strength offers an array of the finest Japanese brands, which have been winning prizes and acclaim worldwide.

A Nikka Single Malt Yoichi offers a fine, smoky yet fruity finish, and can be enjoyed without breaking the bank. Suntory is Japan's other whisky giant. If you're in the mood to splash out, sample the Suntory Hibiki 21 Years Old, which has topped the blended whisky class four times at the World Whiskey Awards, and in 2014 scored 96 out of 100 in Jim Murray's influential *Whiskey Bible*.

Cask Strength; B1F, 3-9-11 Roppongi, Minato-ku; tel: 6432-9772; www.cask-s. com; daily 6pm 'till morning'; map F2

56

Gorge yourself on Japanese cuisine at Gonpachi, the 'Kill Bill restaurant'

Several Gonpachi restaurants dot Tokyo, but there's only one 'Kill Bill restaurant'. The outsized, wooden space in Nishi-Azabu is said to have inspired Quentin Tarantino in devising the set for his blockbuster film.

Gonpachi Nishi-Azabu looms on the corner of Roppongi-dori and Gaien Nishi-dori; it resembles a *dojo*, or training space for karate martial arts.

Upon arrival, one is greeted by photos of luminaries who've dined at Gonpachi, including George W. Bush. You will be ushered to one of the long rows of dark, wooden tables set on a giant carpet of *tatami* (woven straw) mats – or if you seek more privacy, one of the upstairs booths that look down on the whole affair.

Gonpachi's menu covers the gamut of Japanese cuisine from

sushi to *kushiyaki* (skewers and grilled food) on to noodles, *donburi* rice dishes and tempura. Top it off with a lovely confection like a *kuzumochi* and *kinako* ice cream, a yummy sundae-like specialty that mixes glutinous rice, roasted soybean flour and black sugar syrup – all of which taste far better than they sound.

Despite its status as a Tokyo cliché, Gonpachi is the kind of tourist trap that even the locals love. It's usually packed with Japanese on weekend nights.

Gonpachi Nishi-Azabu; 1-13-11 Nishi-Azabu, Minato-ku; tel: 5771-0170; www.gonpachi.jp; 11.30am–3.30am; map D1

The Global Dining group

Gonpachi is one of several franchises run by the immensely successful Global Dining group. Some of the others are **La Boheme**, which serves decent pasta, and **Zest**, which does a pretty fair take on Tex-Mex. All can be counted on for solid service, English-speaking staff (to a point) and a gregarious atmosphere.

Bar crawl the infamous Roppongi Crossing nightlife district

Roppongi first made its claim on the world's imagination as a seamy entertainment adjunct to nearby US bases in the post-war era. Despite fancy new office towers and artistic aspirations, the area still offers plenty of decadence and debauchery.

Invitations will be forthcoming – often from African touts – to anyone who ventures to the crossing of Roppongi-dori and Gaien Higashi-dori. They mostly attempt to lure men to hostess bars and strip joints, where the potential to be fleeced, or even have your drink spiked, is high. Comely Chinese ladies are also on hand offering 'happy ending' massages.

But Roppongi remains the premier watering ground for the expat community, and plenty of chances are available to safely rub shoulders with financiers, diplomats, *gaijin* (foreigners) on the make and Japanese who prefer an international atmosphere.

Geronimo Shot Bar (7-14-10-2F, Roppongi, Minato-ku; tel: 3478-7449; www.geronimoshotbar.com; map F2) is a tiny but popular native-American-themed shot bar right on the crossing. The bar has a wide-ranging drinks menu, including 'light', 'medium' and 'hard' shots with names to match,

and has been witness, it claims, to some 'truly legendary partying'.

Another standard fall-back is British-themed watering hole **Hobgoblin** (3-16-33, Roppongi, Minato-ku; tel: 3568-1280; www.hobgoblin.jp; map F2). Owned by the Wychwood brewery of the UK, the establishment aims for the polished wood, English experience. It even features a full menu of pub grub from fish and chips to Yorkshire pudding.

Mistral (5-5-1 Roppongi, Minato-ku; www.trainbar.com; map F2), or the 'Train Bar' as it's called for its train carriage-like appearance, is another hoary pillar of Roppongi nightlife. Known for its friendly vibe and menu of '80s and '90s rock classics, Mistral has a bell – don't ring it by mistake as it signifies you're ordering a shot for everyone. There's a sign apprising patrons of the bell's purpose, so you can't say you weren't warned.

Wall Street (3-15-22 Roppongi, Minato-ku; tel: 6804-5416; http://wallstreetcafejp.com; map F2) is a spot where foreign financiers mingle, often with domestic gals on the town. This long-time watering hole offers up expertly mixed drinks and a view of the main Roppongi drag.

If you're from Britain and feeling homesick, **BrewDog Roppongi** (5-3-2

Roppongi, Minato-ku; tel: 6447-4160; http://brewdogbar.jp; map F2) is a taste of home in the Far East. The bar has classic BrewDog decor with a wide selection of craft beers, and kids are even allowed in until 7pm.

Tokyo Sports Café (7-13-8 Roppongi, Minato-ku; tel: 5411-8939; www.tokyo-sportscafe.com; map F2) and the **Hard Rock Café** (5-4-20 Roppongi, Minato-ku; tel: 3408-7018; www.hardrock.com/cafes/tokyo-roppongi; map F2) are two standbys that offer exactly what their names promise.

Finally, should you be seeking a bit of erotic frisson but are rightly concerned by the reports of sketchy establishments, the finely toned cast at **Tantra Tokyo** (3-9-5 Roppongi, Minato-ku; tel: 5775-6533; www.tantra-tokyo.com; map F2) puts on proper pole dancing, burlesque, circus and fire shows.

Six trees

Roppongi means 'six trees'. According to two legends, the trees either represent six types of tree that people collected here in ancient times or six feudal families forced to live in Tokyo by the shoguns.

Absorb an avant-garde performance at SuperDeluxe

Japan is justly renowned for its experimental music and performance-art scene. No one venue does more for it than **SuperDeluxe (SDLX)**.

Envisioned by its architect-owners as a 'a bar, a gallery, a kitchen, a jazz club, a cinema...', SDLX is a large concrete space in which anything avant-garde that Tokyo has to offer could be taking place on a given night. For those who want to delve into Japanese noise music, contemporary dance, improv., experimental electronica or cutting-edge design, this is the place to go.

Celebrating its 15th year in 2017, SDLX was founded by Mark Dytham and Astrid Klein, expat architects who established Klein Dytham architecture (KDa) in Tokyo in 1991, and went on to design some of the city's landmark buildings.

In 2003, they launched PechaKucha Night as an event for Tokyo designers to meet and share their work. SDLX was created partly as a home for PechaKucha, which now runs in more than 900 cities around the globe.

For those into design, PechaKucha's punchy presentations happen monthly; on other nights SDLX could host anyone or anything from a noise-music giant like Keiji Haino to avant-garde *koto*-player (a *koto* is a type of Japanese zither) Michiyo Yagi to a 'Disrupting Japan' podcast-recording session.

SDLX can be found a few minutes downhill from the crossing, next to the Roppongi Hills complex on Gaien Nishi-dori. Enter through a non-descript staircase and find yourself in a world transformed. Entrance charges depend on the night, but the Tokyo Ale craft brews and homemade curries are decent and reasonably priced.

SuperDeluxe; B1F, 3-1-25 Nishi-Azabu, Minato-ku; tel: 5412-0515; www.super-deluxe.com; map E1

Splash out at three Michelin-star restaurant Ryugin

Ever since Michelin shocked the foodie world by giving Tokyo the most stars of any city – in its first look at Japan no less – folks have been arriving for tours devoted as much to Japanese cuisine as to sightseeing. If cost is no object and you're prepared to reserve well in advance, then **Ryugin** is the place to go to experience the apex of modern Japanese dining.

Chef Seiji Yamamoto specialises in *kaiseki ryori*, multiple-course meals (prepare to pay about ¥30,000) made from the finest ingredients sourced from across the Japanese archipelago. Dinners begin with *sakizuke*, an appetiser served with sake, and work their way through *nimono*, a simmered dish; *mukozuke*, a sashimi dish; *hassun*, an expression of the season; *yakimono*, a grilled course; and *shokuji*, a rice dish. Dessert and tea provide the meal's summation.

Courses vary widely depending on the season and availability of ingredients. Yamamoto puts his own spin on each traditional dish. A *chawanmushi* (egg pudding dish) that usually contains chicken may instead have delicate chunks of squid inside. In the spring cherry-blossom season, rice could come flavoured with cherry-

blossom tea and accompanied by *sakura* (cherry) shrimp and chrysanthemum soup, winding up with strawberry and *sakura* ice cream.

A few rules to keep in mind: photography is discouraged, and if you must, only mobile phones are allowed. Perfume and cologne are prohibited. Kids under 10 are also verboten. Ryugin has only 24 seats, a very strict cancellation policy and tourists must reserve via their hotel.

Ryugin; 7-17-24 Roppongi, Minato-ku; tel: 3423-8006; http://nihonryori-ryugin.com; Mon–Sat 6pm–1am; map E2

Discover Japan's leading architects, designers and fashionistas at 21_21 Design Sight

Japan is known for its thoughtful architectural modernism and minimalist chic, and many of its designers are among the world's most influential. A decade ago, architect Tadao Ando and fashion designer Issey Miyake joined forces to create **21_21 Design Sight**, an institution at the Roppongi Midtown complex intended to be the nation's leading design museum.

Ando's sleek concrete building, a low-slung series of wing-like angles that conceal a large underground space, is worth a visit in itself. The museum's name points to the founders' intention to offer a vision beyond 20/20 – to see what is ahead in the future. 21_21 Design Sight doesn't have a permanent collection, so what you'll see depends on what is being shown at the time. But director Taku Satoh has a reputation for hosting con-

sistently challenging and intriguing exhibitions. Recent shows have looked at the career of architect Frank Gehry, and examined the mechanics of motion through simple structures, optical illusions and cutting-edge technology.

If you still have the energy, visit the nearby **Suntory Museum of Art**, which has one of the country's leading collections of traditional crafts and tea-ceremony objects. Or simply step outside into the park and enjoy a quiet moment under the cherry trees before returning to the tumult of Roppongi.

21_21 Design Sight; 9-7-6 Akasaka, Minato-ku; tel: 3475-2121; www.2121designsight.jp; Wed–Mon 10am–7pm; map E2
Suntory Museum of Art; 9-7-4 Akasaka, Minato-ku; tel: 3479-8600; www.suntory.co.jp/sma; Wed–Thur and Sun–Mon 10am–6pm, Fri–Sat until 8pm; map E2

Explore rotating exhibitions in the soaring National Art Center, Tokyo

Among its various world number ones, Tokyo proudly hosts the planet's largest 'empty museum'. Completed in 2007, the spectacular **National Art Center, Tokyo (NACT)** was built not to show off a collection of masterpieces, but to host important exhibitions by modern artists from Japan and the world over. The floor area of the NACT totals 484,376 sq ft (45,000 sq metres), making it Japan's largest museum.

Even if you have zero interest in the current exhibitions, the museum is worth visiting for the building alone. Its signature facet is its curving glass curtain, designed by renowned architect Kisho Kurokawa to draw people in from the street. It does this with flair. Many come simply to sit in the vast lobby and absorb the sun in a comfy chair next to the wall.

While some criticise the 'empty museum' approach, the NACT has hosted numerous key exhibitions, including one on Monet that was the second most visited show of the year, not only in Japan but in the world, in the year of its opening. As a project of the Agency for Cultural Affairs, the NACT also hosts shows by NITTEN, the most influential among the major fine-art organisations in Japan.

Hovering like UFOs above the lobby, the NACT's haute-cuisine Brasserie **Paul Bocuse Le Musee** (tel: 5770-8161) and casual café **Salon de Thé Rond** (tel: 5770-8162) offer excellent drinking and dining options after your art experience is complete.

National Art Center, Tokyo (Kokuritsu Shin-Bijutsukan); 7-22-2 Roppongi, Minato-ku; tel: 5777-8600; www.nact.jp; Wed–Mon 10am–6pm; map E2

SHIBUYA AND EBISU

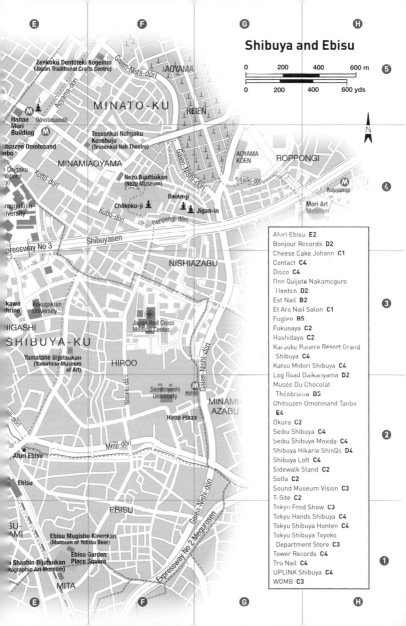

Shibuya and Ebisu

0	200 400 600 m
0	200 400 600 yds

Zenkoku Dentōteki Kogeihin
(Japan Traditional Crafts Centre)

AOYAMA

Hanae
Mori
Building

Omotesandō

MINATO-KU

REIEN

itsuzen Omotesand
nbo

MINAMIAOYAMA

Tessenkai Nohgaku
Kenshujo
(Tessenkai Noh Theatre)

i Daigaku
vations
y)

AOYAMA
KŌEN

ROPPONGI

Seioki-dori

Nezu Bijutsukan
(Nezu Museum)

magakuin
iversity

Chōkoku-ji

Daian-ji

Roppongi

Jigan-in

Mori Art
Museum

xpressway No 3

Shibuyasen

NISHIAZABU

kawa
hrine

Kokugakuin
University

IGASHI

Japan Red Cross
Medical Center

SHIBUYA-KU

HIROO

Yamatane Bijutsukan
(Yamatane Museum
of Art)

Seishinjoshi
University

Hiroo

**MINAMI-
AZABU**

ii-dori

Hiroo Plaza

Meiji-dori

Afuri Ebisu

Ebisu

EBISU

Ebisu Mugishu Kinenkan
(Museum of Yebisu Beer)

SU-
AMI

Ebisu Garden
Place Square

Shashin Bijutsukan
tographic Art Museum)

MITA

Afuri Ebisu **E2**	
Bonjour Records **D2**	
Cheese Cake Johann **C1**	
Contact **C4**	
Disco **C4**	
Don Quijote Nakameguro	
Honten **D2**	
Est Nail **B2**	
Et Ars Nail Salon **C1**	
Fuglen **B5**	
Fukusaya **C2**	
Hashidaya **C2**	
Karaoke Pasera Resort Grand	
Shibuya **C4**	
Katsu Midori Shibuya **C4**	
Log Road Daikanyama **D2**	
Musée Du Chocolat	
Théobroma **D5**	
Ohitsuzen Omotesand Tanbo	
E4	
Okura **C2**	
Seibu Shibuya **C4**	
Seibu Shibuya Movida **C4**	
Shibuya Hikarie ShinQs **D4**	
Shibuya Loft **C4**	
Sidewalk Stand **C2**	
Solfa **C2**	
Sound Museum Vision **C3**	
T-Site **C2**	
Tokyu Food Show **C3**	
Tokyu Hands Shibuya **C4**	
Tokyu Shibuya Honten **C4**	
Tokyu Shibuya Toyoko	
Department Store **C3**	
Tower Records **C4**	
Tru Nail **C4**	
UPLINK Shibuya **C4**	
WOMB **C3**	

Enter a wonderland of sounds at Tower Records Shibuya, the world's largest record store

Mark Twain's quote, 'The report of my death was an exaggeration', nicely sums up the **Tower Records** saga. Though vanished across the West, the once world-beating record chain is alive and well in Japan after local investors bought up what was left of Tower from its 2004 bankruptcy.

For fans of physical media and those who love to browse, a visit to the iconic postmodern building, with its 'Tower Records Orange' accents is a must. With some 800,000 items in stock, the shop is by many measures the world's biggest record store, and it continues to exert an unrivalled influence on Japanese music lovers' minds.

Through the doors, you are greeted by an array of listening kiosks offering a look at the latest releases to hit the shelves. As more than 80 percent of music sales in Japan are domestic sounds, this-ameans loads of J-pop artists like standbys Namie Amuro and Exile, or newer outfits such as Perfume and Radwimps.

Floor Two is the 'Relax' floor, and splits its space between an excellent bookshop stocked with numerous, fascinating music and art-themed books (many in English), and a café in which to browse them.

Floors Three (J-pop, J-Indies), Four (K-pop, soundtracks, anime), Five (rock, new age, club), Six (jazz, soul, R&B, hip-hop, reggae) and Seven (classical, healing) are where the real action is. Pleasingly displayed and loaded with listening kiosks and (if you read Japanese) personal recommendations from staff, these floors are music heaven.

With Japan finally succumbing to digital fever, Tower Records Shibuya may not be there much longer. In the meantime, it's a shrine to physical music culture that must be worshipped at.

Tower Records Shibuya; 1-22-14 Jinnan, Shibuya-ku; tel: 3496-3661; http://tower shibuya.jp; daily 10am–11pm; map C4

Hit world-class nightclubs WOMB, Sound Museum Vision and Contact

From genre-defining beat boxes like the Roland 808 to seminal DJs such as Ken Ishii, Japan has long been central to electronic music. That extends to its clubs, which set the standard for sound quality and a dedicated audience. For dance-music aficionados, a club crawl is a must – and Shibuya is where it all happens. Here are the top three.

WOMB is the dean of the lot. Founded in 2000, this secretive space is entered through a nondescript portal on a backstreet in Shibuya's love-hotel district. As soon as you're inside, however, no expense is spared to engineer the ideal clubbing experience. With room for 1,000 revellers across its four floors, WOMB's repertoire centres on techno, drum 'n' bass and electro. Richie Hawtin is a frequent visitor, and WOMB's line-up of domestic DJs is not half bad either.

If WOMB seems well hidden, then **Sound Museum Vision** – despite its vast size – is even more clandestine. If not for the long line on a weekend night, you'd hardly recognise its entrance on Shibuya's main Dogenzaka drag. One enters Sound Museum Vision through a narrow bar that ushers you onto the sprawling main dance floor. But you're not done yet. A long hallway gives way to two more dance floors, with lounges secreted to the sides. You'll find 1,500 people grooving to house, hip-hop, techno, dubstep and the like on any given weekend night.

The smallest of the three is nearby **Contact**, which despite its modest size has the purest pedigree. Named by techno-legend Derrick May, the club is the spiritual successor to much-mourned Yellow, Eleven and Air and caters to connoisseurs of house and techno.

Hours vary.

WOMB; 2-16 Maruyamacho, Shibuya-ku; tel: 5459 0039, www.womb.co.jp, map C3
Sound Museum Vision; 2-10-7 Dogenzaka, Shibuya-ku; tel: 5728-2824; www.vision-tokyo.com; map C3
Contact; 2-10-12 Dogenzaka, Shibuya-ku; tel: 6427-8107; www.contacttokyo.com; map C4

Savour sushi whizzed to your table on mini trains at Katsu Midori

Conveyer-belt sushi isn't a rarity – but how about a restaurant where sushi is delivered to you on miniature bullet trains? Or how about both? **Katsu Midori** not only has a regular supply of fish rotating through the shop, but you can also order a la carte and minutes later have the sushi of your heart's desire materialise at your table on a tiny train.

Katsu Midori is a popular chain, with branches all over town. Its Shibuya branch, located at the top of the Seibu department store, is perennially crowded, so be prepared to queue as no reservations are taken.

Once you've made your way to the front of the queue, you'll be welcomed with a zesty 'Irasshaimase' (Come in!) and ushered to your table in the brightly lit and lively interior. You can take your pick from whatever happens to be circulating on the conveyor belt, or put your order in via an iPad, replete with comprehensible English.

Katsu Midori's sushi isn't as fresh as the stuff you'll get at Tsukiji, but for a cheap, convey-or-belt chain it's pretty tasty. Begin with the ¥1–200 plates of *nigiri* (fish on rice) and move on to *ikura* (salmon roe) or *uni* (sea urchin) at ¥250, or a finer cut of *chutoro* sashimi (fatty tuna) for ¥350. Complement the fish with a *hiyayako* (cold tofu with scallions and ginger) or a lovely *kani shiru* (crab soup). Then top it all off with a black sesame pudding or coffee jelly.

Katsu Midori Shibuya; Seibu Shibuya 8F, 21-1 Udagawacho, Shibuya-ku; tel: 5728 4282; http://katumidori.co.jp/shibuya; daily 11am–10pm; map C4

While away an afternoon in Shibuya's department stores

Tokyo doesn't have a shortage of department stores. What makes Shibuya ideal for browsing them is that it holds the densest concentration of shops catering to everyone, from ladies who lunch to the young and trendy.

Japan's department stores were often founded by railway companies as anchors for their commuter hubs – it's appropriate that Tokyu's first outlet sits directly atop the firm's Toyoko lines at Shibuya Station. **Tokyu Shibuya Toyoko** (2-24-1 Shibuya, Shibuya-ku; tel: 3477-3111; www.tokyu-dept.co.jp; map C3) offers a basic line-up catering to commuters in a hurry.

Of more interest are **Shibuya Hikarie ShinQs** (2-21-1 Shibuya, Shibuya-ku; tel: 3461-1090; www.hikarie.jp; map D4), which packs a slew of trendy, youth-oriented boutiques and the Orb Theatre into the futuristic Hikarie building on the east side of the station, and the classy **Tokyu Shibuya Honten** (2-24-1 Dogenzaka, Shibuya-ku; tel: 3477-3111; www.tokyu-dept.co.jp; map C4) flagship, down Bunkamura-dori west of the station. The latter caters to the wealthy elite of the nearby Shoto district, and also contains a concert hall and the thoughtfully curated Bunkamura Museum.

Facing Shibuya Station from the north side of the famous Scramble Crossing is **Seibu Shibuya** (21-1 Udagawacho, Shibuya-ku; tel: 3462-0111; www.sogo-seibu.jp; map C4), a shopping paradise catering extensively to women, with overseas brands like Marc Jacobs and domestic designers such as Issey Miyake.

Offering a more varied selection of goods are **Seibu Shibuya Movida** and **Seibu Loft**. Movida (information as Seibu Shibuya, above), caters to rich young fashionistas, with brands like Via Bus Stop. Loft (address and tel as Seibu Shibuya, above; www.loft.co.jp) is a funky lifestyle, interior and stationery citadel with a wide selection of finely designed objects from all over Japan and the world.

Shibuya is also home to the youth-focused Parco, now undergoing a multi-year renovation, and Marui, also catering to the area's young and stylish demographic.

Snag some *washi* paper or a new travel tote at mammoth Tokyu Hands

Japan is justly renowned for its culture of *monozukuri* ('hand-craftsmanship'). **Tokyu Hands** is a temple to the handmade and DIY ethic, making a visit to its Shibuya flagship a joy.

Opened in 1978, Tokyu Hands Shibuya sits at a key corner of Ino-kashira-dori, overlooking the heart of the district's famous Udagawa-cho youth-culture zone. You're just as likely to see art students shopping for materials as couples browsing for home furnishings.

Be forewarned: the complex is a maze. With three connected build-ings whose floors don't quite line up, you'll find yourself a bit lost – but discovering some oddity around the next staircase is part of the fun. Cutting to the chase, here are the most interesting floors.

Take a lift to the top and work your way down. 7B offers models and paper crafts, but it's 6A that's the real *monozukuri* gold mine. This floor is stocked with lovely, handmade *washi* paper – some of it rough-hewn, some of it with swirls of colour – as well as ceramic materials, stones, leather, dying supplies and everything else a DIY fashionista might need.

5C offers a design workshop for hands-on types, while 5A has an exceptional selection of stationery. Keep moving past floors Four and Three (which mainly offer unre-markable home furnishings) to 2C, where you'll find an astounding range of the finest Japanese *hocho* (kitchen knives) – any of these will make an excellent and practical souvenir from your trip.

Tokyu Hands; 12-18 Udagawacho, Shibuya-ku; tel: 5489-5111; https://shibuya.tokyu-hands.co.jp; daily 10am–9pm; map C4

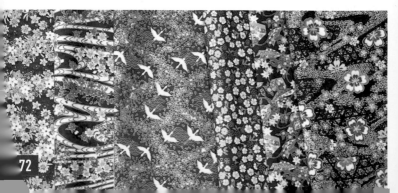

Get your karaoke on Japanese-style at Pasera Resort

When Westerners say 'karaoke', they tend to think 'bar'. But the Japanese will more often think 'room'. This usually means gaudy buildings packed with furnished, private rooms where you and your friends can sing and get sozzled to your heart's content.

A stone's throw from Shibuya Station up Koen-dori, **Karaoke Pasera Resort Grande Shibuya** thinks big, with 10 lavish rooms, an attempt at fine cuisine and even a wine cellar. The building vaguely resembles a casino or nightclub, while the overall aesthetic is 'tropical resort', with aquariums and chandeliers.

Japanese karaoke etiquette

Remember, you're in the country that invented *kara* ('empty') + *oke* ('orchestra'), so when in Rome, do as the Romans do. Should you be sharing the room with locals, don't monopolise the song-selection device. Japanese are all about group activity, so everyone gets a turn, no matter their vocal ability. Restrain your Adele impulses and ensure everybody receives an equal round of applause, too. On the other hand, attitudes towards booze are loose, so it's perfectly acceptable to get totally plastered and fall asleep.

Reservations and menus are available in English, and English-speaking staff are on hand to help you navigate the top-of-the-line karaoke equipment. Despite the pretensions, a night of song (well, two hours anyway) and all-you-can-drink booze comes pretty cheap at ¥4,200 or ¥5,700 per person with set dinner.

Karaoke Pasera Resort Grande Shibuya; B1/B2F, 20-15 Udagawacho, Shibuya-ku; tel: 6415-6035; www.pasela-shibuya.com/ grande; daily noon–6am); map C4

Catch an avant-garde film or binge on falafel at indie movie outpost UPLINK

An independent film distributor, a hotspot with three cinema spaces, a café, gallery and shop, **UPLINK** is a single-destination cultural movement. Since its founding in 1987 by Takashi Asai, UPLINK has shaped Japanese counterculture not only via art films you won't see anywhere else, but by hosting an endless supply of intriguing lectures and concerts.

You'll find UPLINK on a narrow road lined with a fascinating collection of boutiques and cafés. The ground floor is occupied by Tabela, a tasty café with a menu heavy on North African fare. Use the main stairs on the right to enter the cinema and the event spaces.

Recent screenings include emerging 31-year-old director Yoshihiro Sakamoto's *Mashiro no Koi* (Pure White), about a love affair involving a woman with disabilities, and *All Governments Lie*, in which TV news veteran Fred Peabody explores the legacy of maverick American journalist I.F. Stone against the backdrop of Donald Trump's election. You could also take in lectures commemorating the 50th anniversary of the Beatles' 'Sargent Pepper's', or delving into contemporary independent Korean film.

UPLINK is one of the most important alternative voices in Japan, and Asai himself won a key battle over obscenity in art when he successfully fought the government's confiscation of a book of photography by Robert Mapplethorpe, whose work Asai exhibited.

UPLINK; 2F, 37–18 Udagawacho, Shibuya-ku; tel: 6825-5503; www.uplink.co.jp; map C4

National Film Center

Those interested in learning more about Japan's fascinating and influential film history should head to the excellent **National Film Center** (3-7-6 Kyobashi, Chuo-ku; tel: 5777-8600; www.momat.go.jp/english/fc) in central Tokyo.

Eat till you burst at gastronomic paradise Tokyu Food Show

A wonderful and universal feature of Japan's department stores are its *depachika* (basement department) food courts – wonderlands of prepared food and ingredients. For sheer range and convenience, our favourite is **Tokyu Food Show** in the basement of the Tokyu department store beneath Shibuya Station.

Proclaiming itself a theatre of food, Tokyu Food Show caters equally to late-working commuters who don't have time to cook as it does to those in search of the freshest fish and finest fruits for a homemade meal.

The prepared food comes from some of the capital's finest eateries. A stand out is **Pariya**, a delicatessen that specialises in fresh veggie salads, whole grains and imaginative main courses that straddle an intriguing line between Japanese and Western food. They also do otherworldly takes on gelato including *mochi* (rice cake) and *kuromitsu* (black sugar) flavours.

Should you hanker for something that really sticks to the ribs, consider a **Maisen Tonkatsu** sandwich – lovingly breaded deep-fried pork between two pieces of bread with sauces and seasonings.

For desert, consider a pastry at bakery **La Terre** – their Mont Blanc is to die for; or, if in search of something more traditional, buy an *imagawa-yaki* (griddle cake filled with a sweet red-bean paste or custard) from **Tokachidaimyo**.

All the greatest hits of Japanese cuisine from sushi to *yakitori* (skewers) are available, and should you wish to indulge in one of the nation's legendary US$100 melons, **Hayashi Fruits** would be more than happy to separate you from your cash. Alternatively, try one of their luscious persimmons – a fruit not frequently found outside Asia.

Tokyu Food Show; B1F, 2–24–1 Shibuya, Shibuya-ku; tel: 3477-3111; daily 10am–9pm; map C3

Browse swish Daikanyama and top up with lunch at trendy Log Road

In a city of fashionable neighbour-hoods, Daikanyama possibly tops the list. Sandwiched between the hubs of Shibuya and Ebisu, the area is both quiet and highly convenient. Swanky homes for Tokyo's upper echelons and foreign consulates provide the backdrop for swish boutiques, cafés and nightspots.

A good place to start is **T-Site** (17-5 Sarugakucho, Shibuya-ku; tel: 3770-2525; http://real.tsite.jp/daikanyama/english/index.html; map C2), a vast bookshop complex designed by the award-winning architects at Klein Dytham. Peruse six categories from travel to food and drink, architecture and design, or have personalised stationery gifts embossed with same-day monogramming.

For music lovers, **Bonjour Records** (24-1 Sarugakucho, Shibuya-ku; tel: 5458-6020; www.bonjour. jp; map D2) is a must. Inside a ramshackle house you'll find clean, contemporary lines and a fastidi-ously curated collection of vinyl and CDs alongside hip tees and slim-cut sweaters from Maison Kitsuné.

Japan's reputation for quality denim is no longer restricted to the cognoscenti. **Okura** (20-11 Sarugaku-cho, Shibuya-ku; tel: 3461-8511; www.hrm.co.jp/okura; map C2) employs indigo dying techniques that date back to the 10th century, and offers a spec-trum of T-shirts, jackets and – of course – denim, all of it housed in an atmospheric old building.

Top off your shopping at **Log Road Daikanyama** (13-1 Daikanyama, Shibuya-ku; www.logroad-daikan-yama.jp; map D2), a cutting-edge urban complex built in the rail bed of the Toyoko line, which was recently relocated underground.

Crafted from fine wood and me-ticulously landscaped with gardens and trees, Log Road offers a tranquil respite from the metropolitan mad-ness. Enjoy a brew at **Spring Valley Brewery**, but save your appetite for the outstanding baked goods and entrees on offer at **Garden House Crafts**, a café serving Californian plates and grain bowls made from locally sourced ingredients.

Drink sublime coffee and cocktails among the digerati at Nordic hangout Fuglen

Tomigaya, a residential area north of Shibuya Station, is currently one of Tokyo's trendiest areas. The quiet backstreets between the station, Yoyogi Park and busy Yamate-dori are filling up with hipster cafés, bars and boutiques. It's the supreme district for lounging and people watching, and **Fuglen** seems to be the centre of it all.

This café, vintage showroom and cocktail bar is the Tokyo outpost of its mothership in Oslo, Norway (fuglen means 'bird' in Norwegian). Opened in 1963, the original Oslo shop is viewed as a paragon of mid-century Scandinavian design, which in turn was deeply influenced by Japan's minimalist aesthetic. This explains the owners' wish to, in a sense, return to their roots.

The Tomigaya Fuglen inhabits the ground floor of a lovingly restored home that looks onto a pedestrian path, allowing for maximum chilling on benches that line the exterior. Inside, you'll find a carefully curated selection of mid-century sofas, tables and lamps (available to buy), and a counter bar that suggests bachelor pad more than café.

It should come as no surprise that folks here take their coffee seriously. During the day, Fuglen serves to-die-for espresso-based drinks, Kalita drip and AeroPress coffee made from beans flown in from the finest Oslo roasteries. By night, sip original cocktails such as a ravishing ginger Daiquiri alongside the beautiful people.

Fuglen; 1-16-11 Tomigaya, Shibuya-ku; tel: 3481-0884; www.fuglen.com; hours vary, see website; map B5

Stroll the scenic Meguro River and visit its trendy shops and cafés

If you have the good fortune to visit Tokyo during cherry-blossom season, the Meguro River is one of the loveliest spots in Tokyo to enjoy the pink blooms, particularly at night when lanterns create a magical scene. In recent years, businesses along the river have also sponsored ambitious LED illuminations in winter. And in any season, the river, overhung with 800 trees and bounded on either side by trendy boutiques and eateries, is one of the best places in the capital for a lazy stroll.

Meguro River itself is really nothing more than a concrete-encased stream that runs about 5 miles (8km) into Tokyo Bay through Setagaya, Meguro and Shinagawa wards. But the extensive greenery and commerce that have grown up around the channel in one of Tokyo's hippest sections give it an undeniable allure.

The sweetest stretch of the Meguro lies between Naka-Meguro Station on the Hibiya and Tokyu Toyoko lines (two stops from Shibuya) and Ikejiri-ohashi Station on the Shin-Tamagawa line (one stop from Shibuya). This 1-mile (1.5km) section runs through the Aobadai area, one of Tokyo's poshest residential districts.

The Meguro River is best reached from Naka-Meguro Station. Exit the station, walk northeast for less than 330ft (100 metres) and you will soon find the river. Turn northwest (left) to walk towards Ikejiri-ohashi.

Fill up for your walk close to the station at **Hashidaya** (1-15-8 Kami-Meguro, Meguro-ku; tel: 6278-8248; www.hashidaya.com; map C2), where windows offer views of the esplanade while you dine on charcoal-grilled free-range chicken or hot pot.

Slightly back towards Naka-Meguro and on the far side of the river is a dessert spot of some local renown, **Cheese Cake Johann** (1-18-15 Kamimeguro, Meguro-ku; tel: 3793-3503; http://johann-cheesecake.com/ja; map C1), which does a wonderfully light take on the classic.

Top it off by recaffeinating at **Sidewalk Stand** (1-23-14 Aobadai, Meguro-ku; tel: 5784-2747; http://sidewalk.jp; map C2), a welcoming café, craft brew and sandwich nook another 330ft (100 metres) or so from Naka-Meguro.

Meander along towards Ikejiri-ohashi. Should you conduct your stroll in the evening, **Solfa** (20-5-1 Aobadai, Meguro-ku; tel: 6231-9051;

www.nakameguro-solfa.com; map C2) is a funky nightclub just north of the river. DJs spin the latest sounds from house to dubstep to revellers on two smallish dance floors; or simply survey the scene while you appreciate a brew at the bar.

Should you be in the mood for something more traditional, **Fukusaya** (1-26-7 Aobadai, Meguro-ku; tel: 3793-2938; www.fukusaya. co.jp; map C2) is a Japanese confectionary specialising in *castella*, a kind of sponge cake that was brought to Japan by Portuguese merchants in the 16th century, but that the locals have made completely their own.

For a break from the hip urbanity of the Meguro River, a short walk south of the river will bring you to roaring Yamate-dori and the headquarters of **Don Quijote** (2-19-10 Aobadai, Meguro-ku; tel: 5725-7532; www.donki.com; map B2). The pioneer of discount shopping in Japan, Quijote is a garish cornucopia of everything from bicycles to bananas.

A few minutes further along the Meguro River will bring you near your destination of Ikejiri-ohashi Station.

Sample Japan's fanciest chocolate confections at Musée Du Chocolat Théobroma

The foodie press is full of tales of Japanese who go to Europe and ... its culinary arts, only to ... their one-time teachers. ... master Koji Tsuchiya ... in Paris with the ... and his **Musée** ... **roma** brings ... se atten- ... French

You'll find Théobroma further north of café Fuglen (see page 77) from Shibuya along the main Kamiyama *shotengai* (shopping street), not far from Yoyogikoen Station. The glass-fronted facade offers passersby maximum temptation by showing off the various confections in their cases. In keeping with Tsuchiya's background, Théobroma's chocolate truffles are French inspired: you'll find plenty of liqueur options, as well as those based on hazelnuts and fruits. Interesting conserves are also on offer here, including kiwi jam and chocolate, orange and banana spread. In the corner is a small café area where you can sip the smoothest, richest hot chocolate in all of Japan.

Théobroma also has branches in Ikebukuro and inside the Shinjuku Odakyu department store. Recently they've diversified into gelato, offering superb takes on the Italian ice cream at shops in Yoyogi not far from the main chocolate shop, as well as in Kagurazaka in central Tokyo.

Musée Du Chocolat Théobroma; 1-14-9 Tomigaya, Shibuya-ku; tel: 5790-2181; www.theobroma.co.jp; daily 9.30am–8pm; map B5

Enjoy the finest rice Japan has to offer at serene Ohitsuzen Tanbo

The Japanese are justly proud of their succulent rice (a quality they share with many of their Asian neighbours, despite the different flavours). **Ohitsuzen** (meaning 'wood rice container') **Tanbo** (meaning 'rice paddy') grow their own rice in far-off Niigata Prefecture, delivering it to a trio of outlets in the Shibuya and Shinjuku area fresh from the paddy. Of the three, the Omotosando shop is the most convenient for visitors.

Passing under the *noren* (entry curtain), you'll find yourself in an unassuming wooden space. Hanging above the table is a *jizaikagi*, a large ceiling hook for holding pots above the fire. The gentle strains of shamisen music make the urban hubbub recede until you can imagine yourself at a humble restaurant in rural Niigata itself.

The menu at Ohitsuzen Tanbo adheres to the pure essentials of premodern, pre-Westernised Japanese food. Choose from several *ohitsuzen* platters. These consist of a container of freshly milled rice, a small item of protein – mostly grilled fish including salmon and mackerel, though pork and chicken are available – *akadashi* (miso soup), Japanese pickles and brown-rice *chazuke* (tea). For those in a hurry or on a budget, the most divine, moist and chewy *onigiri* (rice balls) are available with stuffing including eel, salmon roe, *konbu* (seaweed) and more.

Ohitsuzen Tanbo; 5-49-5 Jingumae, Shibuya-ku; tel: 3320-0727; daily 11am–11pm; map E4

Get your nails sculpted into 3D masterpieces of art

Japan has adopted and co-opted many Western approaches to beauty. Nail art is one area where the nation's sophisticated aesthetics and attention to detail have combined to produce the world's most advanced practitioners. While in Shibuya, why not get your nails transformed into tiny seasonal or even anime-themed creations to show off back home? Here are some of the area's more intriguing salons.

The nail artists at **Est Nail** (1-20-2 Aobadai, Meguro-ku; tel: 5456-4870; map B2) in über-hip Nakameguro will transform your nails into looks ranging from 'simple office' to 'girly date', or if you're really feeling extroverted, 'casual pop'. Choose from a range of lacquers and decorations from stones to airbrushing.

Also in Nakameguro, find the tiny but charming **Et Ars Nail Salon** (2-43-4 Kamimeguro, Meguro-ku; tel: 6451-0993; map C1), where skilled artist Ran Inoue will convert your nails into canvasses on which she will apply masterpieces by Van Gogh, Klimt or any painter whose work you should happen to fancy.

If you're into something a bit more punk, **Disco** (1-14-9 Jinnan, Shibuya-ku; tel: 3464-7813; www.disco-tokyo.com; map C4) nail salon in Shibuya is a place where your imagination is the limit. Nailist Nagisa Kaneko will render graffiti or abstract art onto your nails, or apply any image of your choosing depending on your taste and budget.

Also in Shibuya, **Tru Nail** (1-20-12 Jinnan, Shibuya-ku; tel: 6416-9709; map C4) is an over-the-top experience with branches across Japan. The emphasis here is on personal consultations, and the nail artists will give consideration to your lifestyle and the condition of your nails.

At ¥8–15,000, sculptures don't come cheap, but they will be among the most durable nails you've ever had.

Taste-test the new style of lighter ramen sweeping across Japan at Afuri

While the traditional heavy *tonkotsu* (pork ramen) crowds the West, the Japanese are busy exploring lighter interpretations of the dish. **Afuri** is at the vanguard, offering fresh recipes that explore the potential for the noodle to coexist with less-calorific yet still aromatic broths.

With 10 outlets (including a new one in Portland, Oregon), Afuri has clearly struck a chord since opening its first outlet at the foot of Mount Afuri, west of Tokyo, in 2001. Legend holds that Mount Afuri is father of Mount Fuji, and the peak has long been known for its clean waters. We like the airy main outlet in Ebisu, which also affords the chance to explore this buzzing district.

The key to Afuri's ramen is a broth centred around the piquant flavour of yuzu, a small yellow citrus native to East Asia with a more complex flavour and aroma than lemon. The yuzu is mixed into a chicken-based broth and sprinkled on top for good measure. Choose from among yuzu *shio* (yuzu-salt) or yuzu *shoyu* (yuzu-soy) ramen, or if you're feeling bold try a spicy yuzu *ratanmen* or *tsukemen*, in which the noodles are dipped into the broth which

comes separately. There is also a rare vegan ramen, and three different types of noodles to choose from depending on whether you like them thin and delicate or thick and chewy.

Afuri Ebisu; 1-1-7 Ebisu, Shibuya-ku; tel: 5795-0750; http://afuri.com; daily 11am–5am; map E2

83

HARAJUKU, OMOTESANDO AND AOYAMA

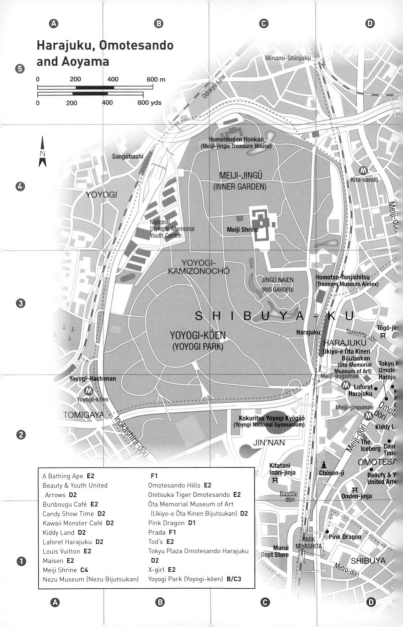

Harajuku, Omotesando and Aoyama

0 200 400 600 m
0 200 400 600 yds

N

Minami-Shinjuku

Odakyu Line

Kita-sandō

Homotsuden Honkan
(Meiji-jingū Treasure House)

Sangūbashi

MEIJI-JINGŪ
(INNER GARDEN)

YOYOGI

Meiji Shrine

National Olympic Memorial Youth Centre

YOYOGI-KAMIZONOCHŌ

JINGŪ NAIEN
(IRIS GARDEN)

Homotsu-Tenjishitsu
(Treasure Museum Annex)

S H I B U Y A - K U

Togō-jir

YOYOGI-KŌEN
(YOYOGI PARK)

Harajuku

Takeshita-dori

HARAJUKU

Ukiyo-e Ōta Kinen Bijutsukan
(Ōta Memorial Museum of Art)

Tokyu
Omote
Haraju

Yoyogi-Hachiman

Yoyogi-kōen

Meiji-jingūmae

Laforet Harajuku

Omote sando-dori

Meiji-dori

TOMIGAYA

Kiddy L

The Iceberg

Cand Time

Kokuritsu Yoyogi Kyōgijō
(Yoyogi National Gymnasium)

JIN'NAN

OMOTESA

Inokashira-dori

Kitatani Inari-jinja

Chōsen-ji

Beauty & United Arr

Bastille-dori

Onden-jinja

PARK MIYASHITA

Pink Dragon

Marui Dept Store

SHIBUYA

Metro-dori

A Bathing Ape **E2**	**F1**
Beauty & Youth United Arrows **D2**	Omotesando Hills **E2**
Bunbougu Café **E2**	Onitsuka Tiger Omotesando **E2**
Candy Show Time **D2**	Ōta Memorial Museum of Art
Kawaii Monster Café **D2**	(Ukiyo-e Ōta Kinen Bijutsukan) **D2**
Kiddy Land **D2**	Pink Dragon **D1**
Laforet Harajuku **D2**	Prada **F1**
Louis Vuitton **E2**	Tod's **E2**
Maisen **E2**	Tokyu Plaza Omotesando Harajuku
Meiji Shrine **C4**	**D2**
Nezu Museum (Nezu Bijutsukan)	X-girl **E2**
	Yoyogi Park (Yoyogi-kōen) **B/C3**

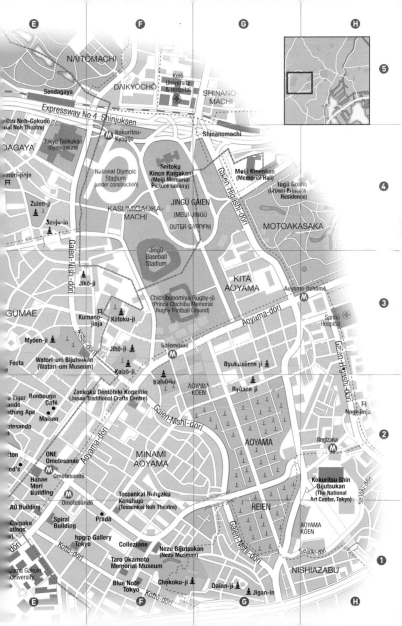

Shop till you drop in the bubbling back streets of youth hub Urahara

Omotosando and Ginza's mostly Western fashion-brand palaces compete to be the world's flashiest, but a stroll down the pedestrian lane called Cat Street that bisects Omotosando offers a more unconventional retail experience. The area called **Urahara** (meaning 'behind Harajuku') is where Japan's most creative designers ply their wares, and Cat Street is the main drag.

Make your way roughly 330ft (100 metres) north from Shibuya Station and veer right onto Cat Street, opposite Miyashita-koen Park. You'll know you're in the right place if you soon spot the lovably garish **Pink Dragon** (B1, 1-23-23 Shibuya-ku; tel: 3498-2577; www.pinkdragon. co.jp; map D1), with its giant golden egg. Housed in a faux Art Deco building, Pink Dragon refracts the 1950s US rockabilly look through a Japanese lens, offering an alternative mix of curios and fashions.

Yuhodo

Cat Street apparently used to be a streambed. Legend says it got its name from the cats that used to wander the street. The official name of Cat Street is Kyu Shibuya-gawa Promenade (sometimes shortened to Yuhodo).

Keep heading north on Cat Street. The first section runs roughly half a mile (1km) to Omotosando. You'll pass a Patagonia shop, after which taller office buildings give way to a funky jumble of older, repurposed homes and shiny new glass shopping arcades housing a range of new and used clothing boutiques, outdoor-wear and accessories shops.

A few minutes past Patagonia, you'll find an outlet of **Beauty & Youth United Arrows** (5-17-9 Jingumae, Shibuya-ku; tel: 5468-3916; www.beautyandyouth.jp; map D2). This national chain curates a selection of fashionable casual clothing of the best quality, and sleek homeware for young urban professionals.

Further north past Burton and Paul Smith on the right, you'll find **Candy Show Time** (6-7-9 Jingumae, Shibuya-ku; tel: 6418-8222; http://candy-showtime.com/cat-street; map D2) on the left. At this popular enterprise you can watch 'candy artisans' make psychedelic Hello Kitty and Pokémon-themed sugar confections.

After passing a final raft of boutiques, you'll arrive at Omotesando, the main avenue through the Harajuku district. Use the pedestrian overpass to cross, and continue past the police box and

Ralph Lauren on your right onto the northern half of Cat Street.

About 150ft (50 metres) east of Cat Street you'll find another alley running off Omotesando that houses large outlets of two of Japan's most iconic brands. Founded by impresario Nigo – a friend and collaborator of Kanye West and Pharrell Williams – **A Bathing Ape** (4-32-5 Jingumae, Shibuya-ku; tel: 5474-0204; map E2) gives the American hip-hop look a distinctly high-fashion, finely manicured gloss that some people just can't live without.

Once a byword for passé in Japan, the second is trainer brand Onitsuka Tiger, which has undergone a startling revival boosted largely by Westerners who discovered its low-tech charms. The castle of trainer delights that

is **Onitsuka Tiger Omotesando** (4-24-14 Jingumae, Shibuya-ku; tel: 3405-6671; www.onitsukatiger.com; map E2) offers (pricey) limited-run Japan-made editions of trainers that you won't find anywhere else.

Continuing north on Cat Street will soon bring you to **X-Girl** (4-25-28 Jingumae, Shibuya-ku; tel: 5772-2020; www.bs-intl.jp/en/shoplist; map E2). First founded by post-punk icon Kim Gordon of Sonic Youth, the shop is now Japanese owned, offering an inimitable Japanese take on rock and punk looks. Just next door is XLarge for men.

Cat Street and its even smaller side streets boast literally hundreds of intriguing shops, restaurants, bars and cafés, so consider this merely a brief introduction. Bring your credit card and get ready to explore!

Gaze at stunning prints of geisha and Mount Fuji at the Ota *ukiyo-e* museum

No one image has done as much to represent Japan worldwide as *ukiyo-e* print artist Hokusai's *Great Wave off Kanagawa*. The piece, with its towering wave threatening to engulf puny boatmen, Mount Fuji in the background, launched a thousand Western imitators, admen and graffiti artists. It's part of Hokusai's series 'Thirty-six Views of Mount Fuji', which can be seen at the intimate **Ota Memorial Museum of Art** in Harajuku.

Founded on the *ukiyo-e* collection of former president of Toho Insurance Company Seizo Ota, the museum occupies a quiet, unassuming building in the backstreets behind bustling Omotosando. Stepping inside ushers you into an oasis of *tatami* (woven straw) mat-

clad calm – ideal for the contemplation of art.

But of course *ukiyo-e* (literally meaning 'art of the pleasure district') were hardly intended to be serene and uplifting – on the contrary these easily reproduced woodblock images were the tabloids of the Edo Period (1615–1868). Images of popular courtesans and *Kabuki* hunks grew so popular that a censorship law was brought into effect in 1790, leading artists to depict less sensational subjects like landscapes. In addition to its first-rate collection of prints by masters including Hokusai, Hiroshige and Sharaku, the Ota museum holds intriguing thematic exhibitions on topics like crossdressers that highlight the risqué nature of some *ukiyo-e*.

An excellent gift shop with a sensitively curated selection of traditional Japanese craft curios like *furoshiki* (traditional wrapping cloths) and chopsticks offers a great opportunity to pick up something for family and friends back home.

Ota Memorial Museum of Art; 1-10-10 Jingumae, Shibuya-ku; tel: 5777-8600; www.ukiyoe-ota-muse.jp; Tue–Sun 10.30am–5.30pm; map D2

People watch on a lazy weekend afternoon in colourful Yoyogi Park

If Central Park defines New York, then **Yoyogi Park** defines Tokyo. In a city devoid of green spaces, Yoyogi – despite its modest size – attracts the full spectrum of humanity that inhabits the world's largest metropolis. If you're looking to get a sense of how Tokyoites relax, this is the place.

Despite its central location between Shibuya and Shinjuku and its overwhelming popularity, Yoyogi Park has only existed since the area – US military housing during the Occupation – was returned to Japan following World War II.

Most people enter from the Harajuku Station side, passing by the gate that marks the entrance to Meiji-jingu and crossing the JR train tracks to the park itself. This route allows you to pass by the gaggle of cosplayers and buskers that ply their trade and attract photo-snapping tourists to the railway bridge.

Once inside Yoyogi Park, make your way to the small ponds that occupy the centre of the park. On a typical warm weekend, the benches and green spaces around the ponds will be occupied by young lovers, families, elderly strollers, dog walkers, foreign tourists – and even a substantial homeless population.

Should you be in the mood for a picnic, several shops and food stalls offer rice balls, hot dogs and drinks. You could also pick up a Frisbee, or even rent a bike and make a full circuit of the park.

If you happen to visit Japan during the end of March to the beginning of April cherry-blossom season, Yoyogi Park will be packed with visitors taking in the cherry blossoms – and getting hammered with friends. As long as you're not causing trouble it's legal to drink alcohol outdoors, and authorities tend to be lenient during the *han ami* (blossom-viewing season).

Yoyogi Park; 2-1 Yoyogikamizonocho, Shibuya-ku; tel: 3469-6081; www.tokyo metro.jp/en/attractions/yoyogi_park; 24 hours year-round; map B/C3

Receive a blessing at serene Shinto shrine Meiji-jingu

Meiji-jingu isn't Tokyo's oldest shrine, but this monument is one of the capital's largest and most important. Emperor Meiji and Empress Shoken are the deities of the shrine. (Their remains, however, are in Kyoto.) The original shrine, built in 1920, was destroyed during World War II; the current shrine buildings were reconstructed in 1958. The shrine itself is made of Japanese cypress.

Most people's experience of Meiji-jingu is limited to a stroll around the grounds. But for as little as ¥5,000, robed Shinto priests will conduct an elaborate purification ritual for you complete with ceremonial ancient dance and music.

Enter Meiji-jingu through the massive wooden *torii* (shrine gate) near Harajuku Station and walk through a stately grove of trees to reach the shrine. You may simply observe the goings on, which often include weddings, or perform a simple prayer at the front. Watch pilgrims bow and clap their hands twice each before making a wish and offering a final bow.

Should you want to go one step further, for a small fee you can buy a small *ema* (wooden tablet) and write your wish on it, or opt for an *omamori* (good-luck charm) or *omikuji* (folded paper onto which an Imperial *waka* poem is written).

Those wishing to take part in a purification ceremony should head to the *Kaguraden* (dance building) to the right of the shrine and ask for a *Yakuharai* (cleansing ritual). This is a common ritual performed to ward off evil, and can be requested for offerings starting at ¥5,000 (depending on the elaborateness of the rite).

Undergoing a *Yakuharai* is a magical way to experience ancient Japanese Kagura dance and music. You will be asked to rinse your mouth and hands and take off your shoes before a priest guides you into the hall. The sounding of a drum marks the beginning of the ceremony.

A purification wand is weaved three times (left, right, left) above your bowed head and priests and shrine maidens then perform a series of chants and dances. The ritual only takes 15 or so minutes, but you will be transported back 1,000 years.

Meiji-jingu; 1-1 Yoyogi-Kamizono-cho, Shibuya-ku; tel: 3379-5511; sunrise–sunset; map C4

Splurge at giant toy emporium Kiddy Land

You can buy anything on the internet, but there's nothing like shopping for Japanese toys in person for getting a sense of the TV, anime and gaming industries behind them. **Kiddy Land** has been the Taj Mahal of Tokyo toy shops for 60 years now, and has had its fair share of celebrity visitors.

Start on the fourth floor, which is divided into zones themed on the Hello Kitty and Rilakkuma franchises. You can pick up select San Rio-produced Hello Kitty goods including play sets and memorabilia for your Kitty fans back home. Rilakkuma ('relax bear') is a less well-known addition to Japan's universe of *kawaii* ('cute') characters, and appears on anything from stationery to dishware, backpacks and stuffed animals.

The third floor is a gold mine of boys' toys, represented by Tomica cars and Plarail railway track and train kits, as well as figurines from Japanese monster films and anime hits, and superbly detailed plastic models and remote-control versions of domestic-brand trains, planes and cars.

The second floor has a large Disney section where, as is often the case with large Western brands, you can get an excellent selection of designs produced exclusively for the Japanese market, as well as Dutch artist Dick Bruna's Miffy, a rabbit with cult status in Japan.

The ground floor is stocked with whatever's trendy right now, and a rotating selection of seasonal goods, while the basement is themed around Snoopy.

Kiddy Land; 6-1-9 Jingumae, Shibuya-ku; tel: 3409-3431; www.kiddyland.co.jp/harajuku; daily 11am–9pm; map D2

Behold the starchitecture and window shop on über-fashionable Omotesando

Often called Tokyo's Champs-Elysees for its regal, tree-lined aspect, Omotesando rivals Chuo-dori as the capital's flashiest boulevard. Just over half-a-mile (1km) long, it manages to pack in almost every globally prominent luxury brand into its length. Shops are housed in starchitect-designed showcase buildings that make the avenue a wonder of design.

Spanning a stretch between Aoyama-dori and Meiji-jingu, Omotesando can be accessed from Omotesando, Meijijingue or Harajuku stations. The boulevard was laid out in the early 20th century as an entrance to the recently completed Meiji-jingu (*omote* means 'front' and *sando*, 'shrine road'), and only recently acquired its prominence. Combine a stroll with a visit to some of the other destinations mentioned in this chapter, including the shrine itself (see page 92), Yoyogi Park (see page 91), Cat Street (see page 88) and Kiddy Land (see page 94).

Omotesando really took off as a classy destination with the 2002 opening of architect Jun Aoki's sleek, contemporary **Louis Vuitton** (5-7-5 Jingumae, Shibuya-ku; map E2), sheathed in cool glass and metallic mesh. Built in 2003

on the far side of Aoyama-dori, Herzog & de Meuron's **Prada** (5-2-6 Minamiaoyama, Minato-ku; map F1) is yet more ambitious, featuring a jagged, crystal form.

Toyo Ito's 2004 building for **Tod's** (5-1-5 Jingumae, Shibuya-ku; map E2) is perhaps more striking still, with asymmetrical lines of concrete bisecting concrete planes. Occupying a long stretch of the north side of Omotesando, Tadao Ando's sleek 2005 **Omotesando Hills mall** (4-12-12 Jingumae, Shibuya-ku; map E2) controversially replaced a funky post-war housing development.

Occupying a prominent corner of Omotesando and Meiji-dori, Hiroshi Nakamura's 2013 **Tokyu Plaza** (4-30-3 Jingumae, Shibuya-ku; map D2) is the most recent monument to unbridled whimsy. Enter its shard-like gate and ascend to the rooftop terrace for a beer or coffee and unwind as you survey the scene below.

Come for the world's most lovingly crafted stationery and stay for a coffee at Bunbougu Café

Is it a café, stationery shop or bar...? **Bunbougu Café** is all of this and more. If you're drained from the Harajuku retail madness and need a moment to compose a few postcards and recaffeinate, it's an ideal place to stop.

Opened by wholesale stationer Toukou Bros. in 2012, Bunbougu (literally, 'stationery') is a shrine to paper and penmanship at a time when the written word is increasingly composed of pixels. The shop has a novel concept: for ¥700, 'members' receive a key to desk drawers that hold pens, notebooks, rubbers and other items they can use freely. The approach has proven popular, with thousands of mainly young adults joining up.

Visitors can browse a broad range of stationery goods from Toukou Bros. and other brands. The Bunbougu Café brand pens are of excellent quality and, well, you've really never used a pencil before until you've tried one of Japan's.

Exceptional pastels and crayons, lovely craft and traditional Japanese wrapping paper, superbly sharp and durable scissors, and funky pen cases all make great gifts for people back home.

When you've worked up an appetite shopping, find a table and dine on a reasonably priced menu that runs from smoked amberjack salad to miso-flavoured pork. Quench your thirst with adoringly prepared latté coffees, teas and original cocktails like a 'Love Letter from Mozart'.

Bunbougu Café; B1F, 4-8-1 Jingumae, Shibuya-ku; tel: 3470-6420; www.bun-cafe.com; daily 10am–11pm; map E2

Amble through the peaceful spaces and gardens of the Nezu Museum

Tokyo has many excellent museums, but none offer quite the combination of superb art and tranquil grounds as the **Nezu Museum**. Built on the estate of Kaichiro Nezu, the railway magnate whose collection forms its basis, the museum offers a peaceful respite from the commercial hubbub around.

The Nezu exhibits approximately 7,400 works spanning painting to calligraphy, sculpture to ceramics, bamboo crafts to textiles. Nezu was himself an ardent practitioner of Japan's tea ceremony, which means that delicate teaware holds a key place amid the museum's seven designated 'National Treasures', 87 'Important Cultural Properties', and 94 'Important Art Objects'.

The museum was rebuilt in 2009 following a design by Kengo Kuma, the architect behind the new national stadium under construction for the 2020 Tokyo Olympics. Kuma's plan is a masterpiece in Japanese *wabi-sabi* aesthetics (finding beauty in transience and imperfection); strolling its serene spaces feels like entering a modern take on a Zen temple.

Its collection isn't as large, but the Nezu is a more manageable experience for viewing traditional Japanese art than the Tokyo National Museum in Ueno (see page 122). Among its must-see masterpieces are the Shinto-Buddhist painting *Nachi Waterfall* from the 13th century, and Ogata Kōrin's gold-leaf screen *Irises* from the 18th century, both designated 'National Treasures'.

Don't leave the Nezu without strolling around its placid garden, a perfect sanctuary of greenery designed in the *shinzan-yukoku* style, with features including pastoral buildings and a teahouse.

Nezu Museum; 6-5-1 Minamiaoyama, Minato-ku; tel: 3400-2536; www.nezu-muse.or.jp; Tue–Sun 10am–5pm; map F1

Get a *tonkatsu* fix at one of Japan's most renowned eateries, Maisen

One side of Japanese cuisine is light and subtle; at the other end are stomach-filling feeds like the fried pork cutlets called *tonkatsu*. Occupying the atmospheric space of a Western-styled World War II bathhouse, **Maisen**, located off Omotesando, is renowned for its fastidious approach to the dish.

Try to get seated in the airy, wood-panelled main dining room, which has a pretty pond. Stay conservative with a *kurobuta* (black pig) fried pork cutlet on rice *(katsudon)* set for ¥1,580, or splurge on the legendary *okita kurobuta* – fried pork loin meal – which at ¥3,780 is still a fraction the price you'd pay for top-line sashimi or *kaiseki ryori* (a multi-course Japanese meal). The satisfyingly crispy, non-greasy

batter coating gives way to juicy, perfectly done meat with just the right amount of umami richness. The sets come with their special *tonkatsu* sauce, and are served with a bowl of rice, miso soup, a large mound of cabbage and a slice of melon to finish it off.

Don't fret if you're not a meat eater. Maisen does the tastiest *ebi* (shrimp) or mixed seafood katsu sets, the latter of which features wonderful shrimp cream croquettes served with homemade tartar sauce.

If you can't make the Aoyama branch, Maisen has other Tokyo outlets including ones in central Tokyo.

Maisen; 4-8-5 Gingham, Shibuya-ku; tel: 3470-0071; http://mai-sen.com; daily 11am–10pm; map E2

Survey the scene and sip a cuppa atop fashion fortress Tokyu Plaza

Roppongi Hills, Midtown, Ginza Six... a central feature of Tokyo's evolving landscape are the urban malls that combine shopping, dining and drinking in aspirational buildings that try to outdo each other in luxury and architectural pizazz.

Tokyu Plaza Omotesando Harajuku sits at the corner of Omotesando and Meiji-dori, one of the capital's most desirable plots of land. Its gleaming, high-tech exterior gives way to a 'theme park' of fashion. Inside you'll find cutting-edge domestic brands from Renai Keikaku to Kimono to Cheek, alongside overseas stalwarts such as Tommy Hilfiger.

Tokyu Plaza encourages you to linger with a Starbucks and Thai-style food stand on the sixth floor, and on the seventh floor a casual yet stylish restaurant/bar called **bills** (http://bills-jp.net). That stands for Aussie Bill Granger, who's created a small empire of restaurants in Sydney, Seoul, Tokyo, Honolulu and London.

But the real charm of this bold statement from the Tokyu railway's department store division is its rooftop. Here is a broad urban park in the sky called **Omohara Mori** (Omohara being a combination of 'Omotesando' and 'Harajuku', and Mori meaning 'woods'). Peer down with a perfect eagle's-eye view on the action at one of the country's trendiest crossings, or gaze out over the Shibuya skyline.

After a hard day's shopping and indulging in Omotesando, Harajuku and Aoyama, this is the ideal perch from which to consider your haul of loot and plan your next foray.

Tokyu Plaza Omotesando Harajuku; 4-30-3 Jingumae, Shibuya-ku; tel: 3497-0418; http://omohara.tokyu-plaza.com; daily 8.30am–11pm; map D2

99

Immerse yourself in Japanese cute culture at Kawaii Monster Café

Ever since Gwen Stefani introduced the world to her Harajuku Girls, the riotous, over-the-top, DIY style developed by denizens of Harajuku has become synonymous with the Japanese word *kawaii* or 'cute'. Fashion impresario Sebastian Masuda, who helped launch the look with his 6%DOKIDOKI shop in Harajuku almost 20 years ago, packaged the experience into a themed restaurant called the **Kawaii Monster Café** in 2015. It's a tacky, touristy experience in the best sense of the words.

A hallucinogenic cake-shaped merry-go-round is the centrepiece of the fourth-floor café, which is divided into four spaces designed by Masuda. At the 'Milk Stand', giant baby bottles hang from the ceiling and huge rabbit, sheep and unicorn heads look down on you. The 'Bar Experiment' is a counter bar guarded by a giant jellyfish. The 'Mel-Tea Room' situates you inside an ice-cream parfait, while the fuchsia 'VIP Pinkcatroom' is for private parties.

The ¥500 entrance fee grants you 90 minutes of psychedelic fun, but food and beverages are extra. Harajuku Monster girls escort you to your seats, where you'll choose from specialties like the colourful 'poison parfait' or the multihued 'rainbow Pasta'.

At night the Monsters stage *kawaii* dance performances on top of the crazy carousel to pounding J-pop and a light show. The girls will invite you to join them on the carousel for a dance – join them if you dare.

Kawaii Monster Café; 4-31-10 Jingumae, Shibuya-ku; tel: 5413-6142; http://kawaii monster.jp; daily 11.30am–4.30pm and 6–10.30pm; map D2

Discover what Japan's trend-defining *gyaru* (girls) are buying at Laforet Harajuku

Tokyo has been overwhelmed by department stores trying to one up each other. And yet, for those in search of *kawaii* ('cute') culture and Japanese fashions you won't find anywhere else, **Laforet** remains the ultimate pilgrimage.

Opened in 1978, Laforet is a six-storey slab of geometric forms that looks increasingly distinctive amid Tokyo's multiplying ranks of steel-and-glass towers. If you don't wish to be overcome by waves of teenage girls, try visiting on a weekday.

The top three floors target young professionals, and as such tend to have more conventional brands like Olive des Olive, As Know As Pink and Pageboy. Further down is where the looks get really interesting. **Laichi** integrates Western designs into Japan-made clothing for one-of-a-kind pieces. You can also choose from wonderfully imaginative silk-screened stockings and patterned ties.

The Goth-Lolita look is integral to Harajuku style, and you'll find a number of shops devoted to it on the B1.5 to B1 floors. **Axes Femme** delivers a neo-psychedelic Victorian take on the theme, all frills and frocks. **Abilletage** is famed

for its wide selection of corsets, petticoats and blouses. If your taste runs more to vampires and witches, this is the place.

Laforet Harajuku also contains two floors of **Store by Nigo**, with the iconic t-shirts and streetwear by the eponymous Japanese designer known for his collaborations with Kanye West, Pharrell Williams and other hip-hop luminaries.

Laforet Harajuku; 1-11-6 Jingumae, Shibuya-ku; tel: 3475-0411; daily 11am–9pm; map D2

SHINJUKU AND IKEBUKURO

Shinjuku and Ikebukuro

A **B** **C** **D**

5 0 200 400 600 m
0 200 400 600 yds

MINAMI-NAGASAKI

Mejiro-dōri

NAKA-OCHIAI

SHIMOOCHIAI

OTOMEYAMA KŌEN

Yakuō-in

Shin-Mejiro-dōri

Shimoochiai

NAKAI

Seibu Shinjuku Line

Nakai

4 OCHIAI KŌEN

Koun-ju Ganshō-ji

KAMIOCHIAI

OCHIAI CHŪŌ KŌEN

Waseda-dōri

Takadam

Takadan

KAMITAKADA

Yamate-dōri

Ochiai

TAKADANOBABA

Suwa-dōri

NAKANO

Higashi-nakano

Higashi-Nakano

Otakibashi-dōri

TOK

Un

3 HIGASHI-NAKANO

NAKANO-KU

KITA SHINJUKU KŌEN

HYAKUNINCHŌ

Tokyo Globe

ŌKU

SHINJUK

Umewaka Nūh Theatre

Hikawa-jinja

Ōkubo-dōri

KITASHINJUKU

Ōkubo-dōri

Ōkubo

Shin-Ōkubo

Ōkubo-dōri

CHŪŌ

Kanda

Shōkai-dōri

KABUKICH

2
Albatross G **D2**
Arty Farty **E1**
Bar Plastic Model **D2**
Bingoya **F2**
Campy! Bar **E1**
GB **E1**
Hotel Chinzanso Tokyo **G4**
Izakaya Asadachi **D2**
Kabuto **D2**
Kinkantei **E1**
Map Camera **C1**
NTT InterCommunication Center
  B1
Robot Restaurant **D2**
Samurai Museum **D2**
Tachibana Shinsatsushitsu **D2**
Tokyo Opera City Art Gallery **B1**
Yodobashi Camera Shinjuku West
  Main Store **D1**
Zauo **C1**

Naruko Tenjinsha

Ome-kaidō

Nishi-shinjuku

Jōen-ji

Seibu-Shinjuku

Sam Muse

Tachiba Shinsats

Tokyo Ika Daigaku Byōin
(Tokyo Medical College Hospital)

Sompo Bijutsukan
(Seiji Togo Memorial Sompo
Japan Museum of Art)

Izakaya Asadachi

Robot Restaurant

Albatross G

Jōfū-ji

Kabuto

Bar Plasti

Shinjuku-nishiguchi

Kinokun

Shinjuku-nishiguchi

Kumano-jinja

Shinjuku Sumitomo Building

Odakyu Dept Store Shinjuku

Bicqlo

Is

Honan-dōri

Kōen-dōri

Tochōmae

Map Camera

Odakyu Shinjuku

Shinjuku

Sh sar

1
SHINJUKU CHUŌ PARK

Tokyo Tochō
(Tokyo Metropolitan
Government Office)

Yodobashi Camera
Shinjuku West Main
Store

Zauo

NISHI SHINJUKU

NTT InterCommunication
Center
Tokyo Opera City Art Gallery

YOYOGI

SHIBUYA-KU

SENDA

Yoyogi

A **B** **C** **D**

Carouse and make friends at the warren of tiny ramshackle bars called Golden Gai

As Japan modernises its cities in the name of convenience and quake resistance, areas that hark back to its more ramshackle past are being viewed with increasing affection. **Golden Gai** ('Golden District') is a six-block warren that has mysteriously evaded the wrecking ball since its tiny buildings were slapped up in the pell-mell post-war years. These days, Golden Gai is a maze of some 200 miniscule bars, many of them visited by writers, artists and actors.

While you can pop into any place that seems welcoming, **Albatross G** is one of Golden Gai's most revered establishments. With three floors, it's a veritable department store of bars by the area's standards. Albatross's calling card is its extensive music collection and laid-back atmosphere. For hipsters and indie-rock types, this is the place.

Another musically intriguing spot is **Bar Plastic Model**. With a collection that spans new wave to anime songs, the bar is a temple of 20th-century bric-a-brac. Gundam and Doraemon figurines nod to local culture, while items like Rubik's cubes signify Western influence.

Tachibana Shinsatsushitsu, or Tachibana 'examination room' offers an unusual take on the bar concept. Bartenders in nurses' uniforms prepare cocktails with names like *Chounai Senjou* ('Colonic Irrigation'); the walls are hung with biology diagrams and skeletons.

Albatross G; 5th Avenue, 1-1-7 Kabukicho, Shinjuku-ku; tel: 3203-3699; www.alba-s. com; Sun–Thur 8pm–5am, Fri–Sat until 7am; map D2

Bar Plastic Model; G2 Street 1/F, 1-1-10 Kabukicho, Shinjuku-ku; tel: 5273-8441; www.plastic-model.net; Mon–Sat 8pm–5am, Sun until 2am; map D2

Tachibana Shinsatsushitsu; 3rd Street 2/F, 1-1-8 Kabukicho, Shinjuku-ku; tel: 3208-4148; Mon–Sat 8pm–4am, Sun 4pm–midnight; map D2

Table charges

Be prepared to pay about ¥1,000 to cover the table charge at most Golden Gai establishments.

Mix sexy and futuristic at the only-in-Japan dinner show Robot Restaurant

Japan has its high-tech AI robots like Honda's Asimo... and then there's **Robot Restaurant**. The producers reportedly invested US$100 million into what is essentially a sexy cabaret show that climaxes in a series of epic robot battles. The show has become a kitschy must-see on the Tokyo tourist circuit, and a visit also provides a bit of frisson as you navigate Japan's premier red-light district Kabukicho on your way here.

Launched in 2012 to lure a new generation of video game and anime-weaned Japanese youths to aging Kabukicho, Robot Restaurant instantly became an unlikely hit with overseas visitors – in particular after Anthony Bourdain visited for his *Parts Unknown* series.

With success came an infusion of cash, upping the ante of laser lights, smoke, special effects, monster robots and the perky young female dancers that ride atop them. The shift from a predominately local to a foreign crowd also meant the show changed its themes from largely American pop-culture ones to more tourist-friendly Japanese ones. In place of superheroes are psychedelic samurai and futuristic *taiko* (drum) troupes.

At ¥8,000 for a 90-minute sitting at the time of writing, it isn't cheap. But hey, how many times are you in Tokyo? If you're idea of Japan is all Gundam, anime, cosplay, samurai and fembots, this is the show for you.

Robot Restaurant; B2F, 1-7-1 Kabukicho, Shinjuku-ku; tel 3200-5500; www.shinjuku-robot.com; 4–11pm; map D2

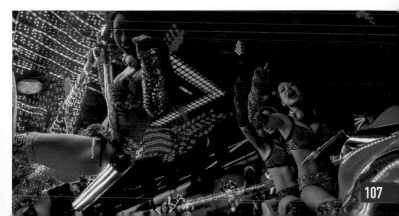

107

Explore five floors of traditional Japanese ceramics, textiles and crafts at Bingoya

Japan is justly renowned for its tradition of *monozukuri* ('handcraftsmanship'). Indeed, the media are prone to go overboard on self-promotion in this regard. Still, if you harbour affection for indisputably superb Japanese crafts, **Bingoya** is the best place in Tokyo to gaze, grasp and ultimately acquire.

Occupying five floors of a building in a quiet corner of Shinjuku

ward, Bingoya sources its objects from across the archipelago. Enter the ground floor and find yourself in a world of Japanese *washi* (handmade) paper, stationery and bamboo products from baskets to flatware, chopsticks, fans, mats and kites.

On floor two you'll discover delicately crafted ceramics that embody Japan's subtle *wabi-sabi* aesthetic of incompleteness and space. Among the items for sale are bowls, vases, earthenware teapots, sake bottles, tea-ceremony objects and glassware.

The third floor is taken up with lovely textiles spanning work clothes and blouses made with traditional indigo dyeing techniques, scarves, cushions and purses.

Floor four ushers you into the realm of *furoshiki* (wrapping cloth), cushion covers, tablecloths, *noren* (entry hangings) and lacquerware of all kinds.

Before you depart, don't forget to pass through the basement, where you'll find an entrancing selection of toys, traditional clay idols, *hirameki* cats and *kokeshi* dolls.

Bingoya; 10-6 Wakamatsucho, Shinjuku-ku; tel: 3202-8778; http://bingoya.tokyo; Tue–Sun 10am–7pm; map F2

Fish from a boat inside Zauo restaurant then have chefs prepare your catch

The Japanese like their fish fresh – so how about a restaurant where you can catch your own fish and have it cooked for you on the spot? That's the appeal of **Zauo**, a lively and perennially popular dinner spot inside the Washington Hotel on the west side of Shinjuku.

Zauo began with the question, 'how fun would it be to have a restaurant where you could fish on a boat?' And that's pretty much the essence of the experience. Enter the restaurant and you will see a wooden 'boat' built above a 'pond' holding a substantial number of fish.

The staff equip you with rods and bait and give you some tips on how to catch your fish of choice. A selection of sea bream, flounder, snapper, mackerel and a few other varieties are available. Snagging your diner isn't so easy, but there are appetisers to keep your stomach from complaining while you work, and should your mission fail you can order from the menu.

With catch in hand, watch the staff fillet and grill it, deep-fry it tempura style, slice it and lay it on rice as sushi, or simply serve it to you straight-up as sashimi.

This being Japan, there's plenty of drama. Staff beat a drum whenever someone lands a fish, and sing a brief prayer of thanks to the creature for giving you its life. Keep in mind that fresh fish doesn't come cheap and reservations are recommended.

Zauo; 3-2-9 Nishishinjuku, Shinjuku-ku; tel: 3343-6622; www.zauo.com; 11.30am–2pm and 5–11pm; map C1

Children's sushi lessons

Zauo offers kids lessons in the basics of sushi making. At the end they receive a Sushi Diploma.

Experience Japan's distinctive gay nightlife in meet-up hotspot Shinjuku Ni-chome

In the post-war era, what was once a red-light district gradually morphed into a place where gay, often married, men could meet males of a similar disposition in discrete bars and clubs. While homosexuality was traditionally not viewed as a sin in Japan, neither was it overtly accepted.

But with the sheer mass of a 30-million strong metropolis making for one of the largest concentrations of gay, lesbian, bisexual, trans and queer people in the world, the small neighbourhood of **Ni-chome** ('two block') has exploded over the years into a maze of hundreds of establishments satisfying just about any taste and de-

mographic. While there's nothing to distinguish Ni-chome architecturally from the surrounding city blocks, you'll know you're in the right place from the profusion of colourful signs, sex-toy shops and of course a multitude of men.

There are spots geared to specific body types, from *gari-sen* (skinny specialised) to *debu-sen* (fat specialised); others target a specific younger or older crowd, and so on.

Notwithstanding the clubby approach of some establishments, there are many that welcome foreigners. **Arty Farty** (2-11-7 Shinjuku, Shinjuku-ku; tel: 5362-9720; www.arty-farty.net; map E1) is a gay dance bar with a mostly male clientele, although an exception is made on Sundays when women accompanied by gay male friends are allowed in.

GB (B1F, Business Shinjuku Plaza Building, 2-12-3 Shinjuku, Shinjuku-ku; tel: 3352-8972; www.techtrans-japan.com/GB/index.htm; map E1) is a men-only venue that is known as one of the favoured spots in Tokyo for meetings between foreigners and locals.

Campy! Bar (2-13-10 Shinjuku, Shinjuku-ku; tel: 6273-2154;

LGBTQ rights

History was made in Japan in 2015, when Shibuya ward in Tokyo became the first municipality to recognise civil unions between same-sex couples. This hatched a trend of local governments giving limited legal rights to LGBT couples. While the movement hasn't trickled up to parliament yet, the tendency towards greater acceptance is clear, and it seems only a matter of time before same-sex marriages are recognised at the national level.

www.campy.jp; map E1) lives up to its billing as celeb drag queen Mlle. Bourbonne and her cross-dressing minions preside imperiously but welcomingly over a candy-coloured interior, promising anything-goes sexuality that makes it a popular cocktail spot for friendly straights as well.

Ending a night of booze with a bowl of noodles is a Japanese ritual and there are few better places to slurp than **Kinkantei** (2-17-1 Shinjuku, Shinjuku-ku; map E1). With 200 years of history, this gem of a shop, instantly recognisable by its black on green sign, crafts thick, al-dente noodles in savoury, steaming broths – and it serves beer too.

Peruse visions of the future at telecom giant NTT's InterCommunication Center

Corporate showcase museums are a mixed blessing in Japan. But the curators at telecom behemoth NTT got things right with their **InterCommunication Center (ICC)** at the Tokyo Opera City complex in Shinjuku. The spacious museum offers two floors of provocative multimedia installations by the best international artists in the field, and a steady diet of worthy exhibitions and lectures. Japan's own Toshio Iwai and American avant-garde artist Laurie Anderson are among the many leaders who have graced this institution.

The ICC is accessed from the fourth floor of Tokyo Opera City. At the entrance to the building, you'll find a gracious lobby, with a quiet, bookshop to your right, and a theatre in the back. Continue up the stairs to the left to enter the main fifth-floor exhibition spaces.

The fifth-floor lobby holds a number of whimsical interactive installations, including the kid-pleasing 'Arts & Science Chronology' exhibit set in the floor, which traces technological developments from the 1900s to the present day. Directly facing you is the main temporary exhibition room, with the permanent installation rooms in the back.

This section, entitled 'Open Space', presents cutting-edge technologies in media artworks including virtual reality and interactive multimedia. Among the immersive installations are Gregory Barsamian's 'Juggler' and the 3D virtual-reality room 'conFIGURING the CAVE' developed by Illinois University's Electronic Visualization Laboratory and the US National Center for Supercomputing Applications. Best of all, everything except the temporary exhibitions are free.

NTT InterCommunication Center; 4F, 3-20-22 Nishishinjuku, Shinjuku-ku; tel: 5353-0800; www.ntticc.or.jp; Tue–Sun 11am–6pm; map B1

Take time out at Hotel Chinzanso, with its tranquil garden

Tokyo has its tranquil gardens, and its luxury hotels, but they only come paired in a perfect package at **Chinzanso**. This complex in the sleepy Mejiro district between Shinjuku and Ikebukuro offers a worthy alternative to more central accommodation – or a nice spot for a stroll and quiet cup of tea.

Seven hundred years ago, the land of Chinzanso was called Tsubakiyama ('Mountain of Camellias'). At the beginning of the Edo era, famous poet Basho Matsuo lived next to the garden. In the Meiji era, a former prime minister came to own the land. He developed the garden with a Kaiyuu-style design encompassing grasslands, a pond, a *Tsukiyama* (earth moulded to look like a small mountain) and winding rivers.

The Four Seasons Hotel Tokyo at Chinzanso opened in 1992, but in 2012 it reverted to simply Hotel Chinzanso Tokyo, with an emphasis on tradition and its rooms' views of the gorgeous garden. Depending on your preference, you can wake up to greenery bathed in morning sunlight, or the skyline of Tokyo spread out before you.

For those merely stopping by, the hotel boasts nine restaurants where you can savour fresh pro-duce from all over the Japanese archipelago. Of special note are **Mokushundo**, which, tucked away in a quiet grove, serves old-style dishes cooked on hot lava rocks from Mount Fuji, and **Mucha-an**, a charming restaurant in the woods famed for tasty soba noodles made from Hokkaido buckwheat. If you're here for dinner, note that last orders are at 8pm.

Hotel Chinzanso Tokyo; 2-10-8 Sekiguchi, Bunkyo-ku; tel: 3943-1111; www.hotel-chinzanso.com; map G4

Delve into Japan's fighting past at the atmospheric Samurai Museum

Deep in the pulsing heart of Japan's largest red-light district – Kabukicho – is a new museum targeting foreign fans of the nation's legendary samurai tradition. The two-storey **Samurai Museum** opened amid much fanfare in 2013, and has drawn mostly favourable reviews for its thoughtfully designed exhibitions that illustrate almost a thousand years of martial history.

The museum is entered on the ground floor, which contains carefully arranged sets of armour from the Muromachi (1336–1573) and Edo (1600–1868) periods.

The second floor presents areas devoted to: the Kamakura period (1185–1333), swords and other bladed weapons, helmets, armour and matchlock guns that evince the samurai's transition to modernity amid interchange with the West.

The museum also offers the chance to view special live-action performances of sword battles by actors, and even an opportunity to have a selfie taken in full samurai armour regalia. For the less martially inclined, there are also calligraphy lessons and a Japanese swords course taught by a former curator of the British Museum.

The installations and accompanying texts elucidate a tradition far more complex than the novice would glean from the occasional Kurosawa flick. For example, while the long Japanese *katana* sword is indelibly linked to samurai in the Western mind, in fact the bow and arrow was the weapon of choice for aristocratic families of the 12th century. The samurai lords of the Edo period we know from Kurosawa's films, on the other hand, rarely experienced any combat whatsoever.

Samurai Museum; 2-25-6 Kabukicho, Shinjuku-ku; tel: 6457-6411; http://samuraimuseum.jp; daily 10.30am–9pm; map D2

Grab the latest gadgets from Japan's electronic powerhouses at Shinjuku Electric Street

Akihabara may be Japan's 'Electric Town', but unless you're building a computer from parts, Shinjuku's Nishiguchi (West Exit) is the handiest place to browse the latest offerings from Japan's electronics titans. A road that extends perpendicular to the station has even taken on the name 'Shinjuku Electric Street' (Denki Gai).

What makes a visit to Tokyo's electronics shops fun is the riot of sounds, bright lights, mini-skirted salesgirls hawking wares and most of all the chance to test out just-released products before they reach the West.

All manner of gadgetry is available, but Denki Gai is known in particular for its camera offerings. That makes Yodobashi Camera a good place to begin your consumer odyssey. Officially titled **Yodobashi Camera Shinjuku West Main Store** (there's another Yodobashi out the East Exit), it's a vast palace of high-tech merchandise. This Yodabashi is actually an agglomeration of structures including Multime-

dia North and South buildings, a Camera building, Game and Travel buildings – and there's even a shop devoted to film photography.

Thanks to the depth of its market and Japanese people's preference for the new, the country is also an excellent place to purchase a used camera or lens. **Map Camera** is the largest of the lot, with six floors offering pre-owned Cannon, Sony and Nikon gear in prime condition available at mind-bogglingly good prices.

Yodobashi Camera Shinjuku West Main Store, 1-11-1 Nishishinjuku, Shinjuku-ku; tel: 3346-1010; www.yodobashi.com; daily 9.30am–10pm; map D1
Map Camera; 1-13-6 Nishishinjuku, Shinjuku-ku; www.mapcamera.com; daily 10.30am–8.30pm; map C1

Bic Camera

For those in a hurry, **Bic Camera** next to Shinjuku Station is also a cornucopia of electronics.

View art by Japanese and international modernists at the Tokyo Opera City Art Gallery

Though eclipsed in size by the Mori (see page 50), MOT (see page 141) and NACT (see page 63), the **Tokyo Opera City Art Gallery** remains a vast 10,000-plus sq ft (1,000-plus sq metre) contemporary art space and one of the capital's leading venues for experimentation. It's Shinjuku's principal art gallery, and along with the NTT InterCommunication Center (see page 112), makes a visit to Tokyo Opera City an attractive proposition.

Despite its name, the Tokyo Opera City Art Gallery isn't a business, but mainly an 'empty museum' along the lines of the NACT, with no permanent collection of its own

but the capacity to host large and impressive exhibitions. Its curators propose that fresh thought and unique viewpoints expressed through art are necessary to counteract the shrinking 'vitality of individual life' caused by Japan's economic growth.

The gallery's curators include some of the freshest voices who have been shaking up Japan's museum scene over the last decade, including Shihoko Iida. Exhibitions have looked at the giant LED installations of Tatsuo Miyajima, the painfully emotional photography of Nobuyoshi Araki, the vibrant multimedia work of Tabaimo and Mika Ninagawa and the fashions of Yohji Yamamoto.

In addition to large-scale temporary exhibitions in the soaring galleries One and Two, there are two further galleries showing the works of emerging Japanese artists and canvasses from the substantial collection of impresario Kotaro Terada, including pieces by Tatsuoki Nambata, one of Japan's most influential abstract painters.

Tokyo Opera City Art Gallery; 3-20-2 Nishi-shinjuku, Shinjuku-ku; tel: 5353-0756; www.operacity.jp/en/ag; Tue–Sun 11am–7pm; map B1

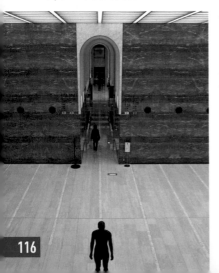

Quench your thirst and test your taste buds in post-war stronghold Omoide Yokocho

If Golden Gai (see page 106) is a historic district that's been buffed by gentrification, **Omoide Yokocho** remains relatively unreconstructed. The fact that its nickname is 'Piss Alley' gives you an idea that it's still a little rough around the edges, but don't let that put you off this atmospheric stretch on the west side of Shinjuku Station.

Omoide Yokocho ('Memory Lane') is in fact a warren of several lantern-lined alleys occupied by numerous *isakaya* (drinking-dining establishments) in hastily thrown-up buildings that are little more than glorified shacks (though many were rebuilt after a 1999 fire). The area is all that's left over from a vast black market that sprung up on the west side of Shinjuku after World War II.

While Omoide Yokocho is of growing interest to tourists, you're likely to find yourself drinking and dining alongside salt-of-the-earth students and salarymen. **Izakaya**

Asadachi (1-2-14 Shinjuku, Shin-juku-ku; tel: 3342-1083; map D2) is a famous restaurant and go-to spot for foreign media in search of 'weird Japan' stories that serves delicacies like raw pigs' testicles and grilled salamander.

If you fancy something more conventional, there are numerous shops purveying the grilled chicken skewers known as *yakitori*. **Kabuto** (1-2-11 Shinjuku, Shinju-ku-ku; tel: 3342-7671; map D2), on a much-frequented corner, was established in 1948 and remains a firm favourite. Stick to *sasami* (white meat) or *tori negi* (chicken leek) skewers for safety, but if you're feeling bold get the *hito-tori* chef's sampler – it could include anything from entrails to eel heads.

Smoking laws

Japan tightened its smoking laws ahead of the 2020 Tokyo Olympics, but small shops like those in Omoide Yokocho were allowed to continue to permit smoking inside.

UENO, YANAKA AND AKIHABARA

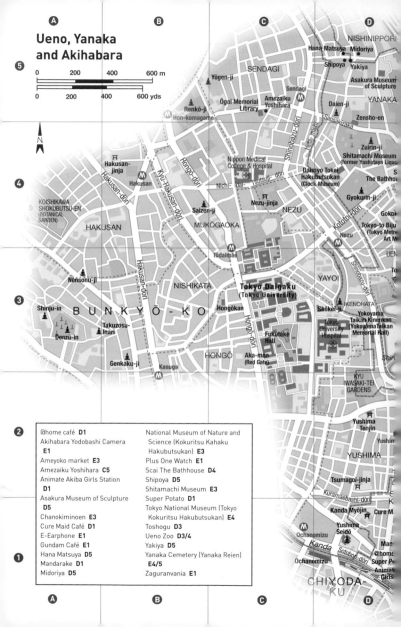

Ueno, Yanaka and Akihabara

0	200	400	600 m
0	200	400	600 yds

NISHINIPPORI

Hana Matsuya Midoriya
Shipoya   Yakiya

Asakura Museum
of Sculpture

YANAKA

SENDAGI

Yōgen-ji

Renkō-ji

Hon-komagome

Ōgai Memorial
Library

Amezaiku
Yoshihara

Sendagi

Daien-ji

Zensho-en

Zuirin-ji

Shitamachi Museum
(former Yoshidaya Liquo

Hakusan-
jinja

Hakusan

Nippon Medical
College & Hospital

Nichi- Idai-   Tsutsuji-dōri

Daimyo Tokei
Hakubutsukan
(Clock Museum)

The Bathhou

Gyokurin-ji

KOISHIKAWA
SHOKUBUTSU-EN
(BOTANICAL
GARDEN)

HAKUSAN

Saizen-ji

Nezu-jinja

Gokok

NEZU

Tokyo-to Biju
(Tokyo Metro
Art M

MUKŌGAOKA

Nezu

UEN

Tōdaimae

Nensonu-ji

NISHIKATA

Tokyo Daigaku
(Tokyo University)

YAYOI

To

Shinju-in

Hongōkan

Shōkei-ji

IKENOHATA

Yokoyama
Taikan Kinenkan
(Yokoyama Taikan
Memorial Hall)

Takuzosu-
Inari

Denzu-in

BUNKYŌ-KO

Fukutake
Hall

Tokyo
University
Hospital

Genkaku-ji

Kasuga

HONGŌ

Aka-mon
(Red Gate)

KYU
IWASAKI-TEI
GARDENS

Shin

Yushima
Tenjin

Yushim

YUSHIMA

Tsumagoi-jinja

Kuramaebashi-dōri

K

Kanda Myōjin

Cure M

Ochanomizu

Yushima
Seidō

Man

@home

Super P

Kanda

Sotobori-dōri

Ochanomizu

CHIYODA-
KU

Anima
Girls

@home café **D1**	National Museum of Nature and
Akihabara Yodobashi Camera	Science (Kokuritsu Kahaku
E1	Hakubutsukan) **E3**
Ameyoko market **E3**	Plus One Watch **E1**
Amezaiku Yoshihara **C5**	Scai The Bathhouse **D4**
Animate Akiba Girls Station	Shipoya **D5**
D1	Shitamachi Museum **E3**
Asakura Museum of Sculpture	Super Potato **D1**
D5	Tokyo National Museum (Tokyo
Chanokiminoen **E3**	Kokuritsu Hakubutsukan) **E4**
Cure Maid Café **D1**	Toshogu **D3**
E-Earphone **E1**	Ueno Zoo **D3/4**
Gundam Café **E1**	Yakiya **D5**
Hana Matsuya **D5**	Yanaka Cemetery (Yanaka Reien)
Mandarake **D1**	**E4/5**
Midoriya **D5**	Zaguranvania **E1**

Be beguiled by the world's most extensive collection of Japanese art at Tokyo National Museum

Japan's contribution to the art world and its enormous influence on Western aesthetics goes without saying. For a concentrated lesson in the development of the nation's art and its inextricable mingling with crafts and religion, **Tokyo National Museum (TNM)** is the place.

Founded in 1872, Tokyo National Museum is Japan's oldest national museum, the largest art museum in Japan and one of the biggest in the world. One could easily spend a full day wandering its six buildings and

not see it all. The museum is located in Ueno Park, so a visit can be combined with a tour of one of the park's other museums, Ueno Zoo or simply a stroll around the park and scenic Shinobue Pond.

If time is an issue, don't miss the Honkan (Japanese Gallery). From the prehistoric Jomon era through the 16–19th-century flowering of Edo-era culture, the Honkan presents ceramics, swords, lacquerware, sculptures, scrolls, paintings, tea-ceremony objects and *ukiyo-e* prints, as well as artefacts of the indigenous Ainu and Ryukyu cultures. The rise of Buddhist devotional art, and the courtly art associated with the Imperial reigns in Nara, Kyoto and finally Edo (Tokyo) contour the narrative of Japan's thousands of years of history.

Should you have more time, peruse the captivating Gallery of Horyuji Treasures. Housed in a sleek structure by Yoshio Taniguchi, the wing displays statuary, *gigaku* masks, sutras and other precious objects from the massive Horyuji 7th-century Buddhist temple in Nara.

More Ueno Park museums
Ueno Park's **National Museum of Western Art** and **National Museum of Nature and Science** are also both well worth a visit.

Tokyo National Museum (Tokyo Kokuritsu Hakubutsukan); 13-9 Uenokoen, Taito-ku; tel: 5777-8600; www.tnm.jp; Tue–Sun 9.30am–5pm; map E4

Stroll the mossy tombstones of historic Yanaka Cemetery

Few parts of Tokyo have been spared the conflagrations, earthquakes, fire bombings and reckless development that characterise the capital's history. Among them, the Yanaka area adjacent to Ueno is perhaps the most charming. This old-fashioned quarter north of the palace dates from the shogunate's decision to fortify the city's periphery with temples that would double as fortresses in the event of invasion.

Yanaka Cemetery, located in grounds surrounding the great Tennoji – a temple that was itself destroyed by fire – is the highlight. The 25-acre (10-hectare) plot contains more than 7000 graves, including a number of political and cultural luminaries, not to mention one of the Tokugawa shoguns. A stroll down its mossy lanes, past worn stone lanterns, offers a rare journey into Tokyo's past as Edo, the capital of one of Asia's wealthiest empires.

Among the graves are those of several distinguished figures. At the graveyard offices, attendants will provide a map and direct you to the last resting places of the composer and blind *koto*-player Miyagi Michio (1894–1956), the botanist Dr Makino Tomitaro (1862–1957), the well-known artist Yokoyama Taikan (1868–1958) and the female

mass-murderer Takahashi Oden (1848–79). Japan's last shogun, Tokugawa Yoshinobu (1837–1913), is buried here too, alongside the destitute whose unclaimed bodies were once requisitioned by Tokyo University as teaching aids.

The best times to visit are spring, when the famous Sakura-dori ('Cherry Blossom Lane') is in full bloom, and autumn, when Yanaka Cemetery becomes a multihued tapestry of autumnal foliage. It's not uncommon to see painters before easels, capturing the flavour of one of the capital's most scenic spots.

Yanaka Cemetery (Reien); 7-5-24 Yanaka, Taito-ku; tel: 3821-4456; daily 8.30am–5.15pm; map E4/5

View pandas at Ueno Zoo and pay respects at Toshogu, shrine to the first Shogun

The nation's oldest zoo isn't its largest, but Ueno Zoo offers an agreeable break from the capital's hustle and bustle – particularly if you're visiting Tokyo with little ones. Top it off with a tour of Toshogu, an imposing Shinto shrine to the first shogun, Ieyasu Tokugawa.

Founded in 1882 on a former Imperial estate, **Ueno Zoo**'s 35 acres (15 hectares) contain more than 2,600 animals from 464 different species including: tigers, lions, gorillas, monkeys, elephants, giraffes, okapis, hippopotamuses, polar bears and a pair of notoriously sex-shy pandas, Lili and Shinshin. Though the zoo isn't the most spacious, efforts have been made to modernise enclosures to suit the ecosystems of the respective species. If you're with kids, Ueno Zoo also has a sizable Children's Zoo petting area where tots can feed sheep, goats and the usual assortment of farm animals.

Adjacent to Ueno Zoo is **Toshogu**, a shrine which memorialises the founder of the Edo Shogunate, Ieyasu Tokugawa (1542–1616), who unified Japan and remains renowned for his martial prowess (and cruelty). Sadly, earthquakes, fires and war have robbed Tokyo of most of its legacy of Edo-era

(1603–1868) buildings. Clad in gold and ornate carvings, Toshogu remains a statement of the shoguns' immense wealth and power.

As you approach Toshogu from the front, you will see a large pagoda on your right. This imposing structure is a remnant of the old **Kan'ei-ji**, the Buddhist temple where six of 15 shoguns are buried. Most temple structures were destroyed in a 1657 fire. Despite being rebuilt, the temple was ravaged again during the Boshin War's 1868 Battle of Ueno and never restored.

Reaching Toshogu, enter through the *Karamon* gate. Dating to 1651, the gate is wrapped in lavish gold foil and decorated with flowers and birds. Two dragons on the gate pillars, the Ascending and Descending Dragons, are said to visit nearby Shinobazu Pond every night to drink from its water.

The shrine itself may be the finest example of Edo-era architecture still standing in Tokyo. All of the pillars and doors are covered in gold foil, and the ceilings decorated with lacquer and colourful carvings. People come to pray to the spirit of Ieyasu Tokugawa and pick up an *omomori* (good-luck charm) or an *omokuji* (fortune slip), which are even available in English.

Finish your day with a stroll by Shinobazu Pond, which is the remnant of marshes that once covered much of Tokyo's old Shitamachi (central/downtown) district. The pond appears in countless artworks and is renowned for its carpet of lotus flowers, birds and its island, with a temple dedicated to the goddess Benzaiten.

Ueno Zoo (Ueno Dobutsuen); 9-83 Ueno Koen, Taito-ku; tel: 3828-5171; www.tokyo-zoo.net/english/ueno; Tue–Sun 9.30am–5pm; map D3/4 Toshogu; 9-88 Ueno Koen, Taito-ku, tel: 3821-3455; www.uenotoshogu.com; daily 9.30am–4.30pm; map D3

Wartime cull
During World War II, Japan's government instructed Ueno Zoo to kill its animals for fear that US bombing would result in freed beasts running amok in the streets of Tokyo. Despite pleas from the zookeepers, the animals were poisoned or left to starve.

Contemplate art in the house of the father of modern Japanese sculpture

Along with Yanaka Cemetery, the **Asakura Museum of Sculpture** sits atop the many charms of historic Yanaka. Called the father of modern Japanese sculpture, Fumio Asakura's work can be viewed in the context of his quaint studio-house not far from the graveyard.

Asakura (1883–1964) inhabited an era when Japan was hastily modernising, and artists were formulating responses to the challenges of Western art. For many, this meant turning away from religious themes to naturalist ones.

Born in far-off Kyushu, Asakura moved to the capital to study at the Tokyo University of the Arts. Apparently he was so poor that he would wander Ueno sketching animals – a proclivity visible in his numerous cat sculptures.

Asakura moved in here in 1908 and remained in the house to his life's end, gradually expanding it with a Japanese-style residence and Western-flavoured studio. The **grand studio** holds several large statues, presided over by a creation of former prime minister of Japan, Shigenobu Okuma.

The upstairs **Orchid Room** is home to a number of superb statues of cats, while higher still is an eye-catching roof garden from which to view the exquisite Japanese garden below and the statues scattered across the roofs.

On the other side of Yanaka, don't miss **Scai The Bathhouse**, a cutting-edge contemporary art gallery built out of a repurposed 200-year-old public bathhouse. Scai represents noted domestic and international artists like Tatsuo Miyajima and Anish Kapoor. With its tiled roof, towering chimney and stolid masonry walls, the gallery makes a pleasingly unconventional space for viewing art.

Asakura Museum of Sculpture (Asakura Chosokan); 7-18-10 Yanaka, Taito-ku; tel: 3821-4549; www.taitocity.net/zaidan/asakura; Tue–Thur and Sat–Sun 9.30am–4.30pm; map D5
Scai The Bathhouse; 6-1-23 Yanaka, Taiko-ku; tel: 3821-1144; www.scaithebathhouse.com; Tue–Sat noon–6pm; map D4

Hunt for electronics in Japan's largest gadget bazaar, Akihabara

Back in the Walkman era, Japan's 'Electric Town' used to be the place for engineers and tinkerers to pick up parts and supplies. These days it's best known as a shrine of *otaku* ('fanboy') culture. But Akihabara still boasts what may be the world's largest electronics shop and some fascinating gadget specialty outlets.

It's hard to find adequate superlatives to describe the **Akihabara Yodobashi Camera** (1-1 Kanda Hanaokacho, Chiyoda-ku; map E1). Words like gigantic and behemoth come to mind when picturing Yodabashi's nine floors of consumer electronics, household appliances and gadgets. Enter on the ground floor near the metro stop and become a human pachinko ball in a giant machine of mobile phones, cameras, computers, AV (audio/video) and household goods.

Akihabara

Akihabara is named for the deity of a shrine built after a fire consumed the area in 1869. It developed as a black-market centre after World War II and gradually shifted to electronics. In 2008, a man drove a truck into pedestrians, then got out and stabbed others, ultimately killing seven in the 'Akihabara Massacre'.

There's even a restaurant floor and a golf-driving practice range.

Should you prefer browsing in digestible-size shops, Akihabara has some other unique offerings. At **E-Earphone** (4F, 4-6-7 Sotokan da, Chiyoda-ku; map E1) you can test out an innumerable selection of headphones, earbuds and other personal audio devices, and choose from among new and used models.

Given Japan's preference for the shiny and new, the country offers steals on used goods in everything from cars to electronics. At **Plus One Watch** (17 Kanda Matsunagacho, Chiyoda-ku; map E1), customers can find solid bargains on everything from domestic brands Casio and Seiko to European fashion statements such as Rolex and Bulgari.

Visit a maid café and come to grips with *moe* culture

While Akihabara was once best known for electronics, it's now more often thought of as the world epicentre of *otaku* ('fanboy') culture. That means an obsession with manga and gaming, and immersion in *moe* – a Japanese term that roughly means an attachment to young, beautiful and innocent female characters. Akihabara's maid cafés emerged to cater to *otaku* fantasies after they'd finished gorging on manga, games and electronics.

Many of Akihabara's maid cafés can be found in and around Chuo-dori, and girls will often be handing out flyers to their establishments. **Cure Maid Café** was reportedly the first maid café ever. Cute girls in frilly maid uniforms attend to customers as they would a Victorian-era lord, while soothing classical music plays in the background. Lunch, dinner and tea service are on the menu, and for those with knowledge of the latest anime and manga, there are regular thematic events based on popular characters.

@home café is perennially popular and offers an experience made in *moe*-maid heaven. The girls chant '*moe moe kyun*' over your drinks, apparently to make them tastier, and will even write a message in ketchup on your omelette rice. They also sing and dance to popular anime numbers.

If you fancy a proper meal, **Zaguranvania** brings the gastro-pub concept to the maid-café experience. Choose from among 30 different beers from 12 different countries (two hours of all you can drink will set you back ¥1,600). They also serve full-course meals for between ¥4,000 and ¥5,000.

Cure Maid Café; 6F, 3-15-5 Sotokanda, Chiyoda-ku; tel: 3258-3161; www.cure maid.jp; Mon–Thur 11am–8pm, Fri–Sat until 10pm, Sun until 7pm; map D1
@home café; 4F-7F, 1-11-4 Sotokanda, Chiyoda-ku; tel: 3255-2808; www.cafe-athome.com/en; Mon–Fri 11am–10pm, Sat–Sun 10am–10pm; map D1
Zaguranvania; 1-14-3 Sotokanda, Chiyoda-ku; tel: 5890-5828; noon–11.30pm; map E1

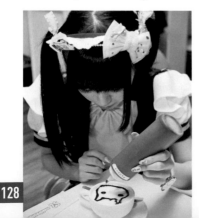

Search for knick-knacks in the Yanaka Ginza, then sink your teeth into Japanese 'B-grade' gourmet

A lively reprieve from Ueno's museums and Yanaka Cemetery is the Yanaka Ginza, a slender shopping street full of temples, small shops, cafés and traditional craft stores redolent of pre-war Tokyo.

Hana Matsuya (3-15-5 Nishinippori, Arakawa-ku; map D5) is a kimono shop dating back to 1891 and a fun spot to browse or pick up a keepsake. Traditional wooden slippers known as *geta* are a popular souvenir, but beware – they take a long time to break in!

Midoriya (3-13-3 Nishinippori, Arakawa-ku; map D5) has specialised in bamboo crafts made by hand since 1908. Traditional baskets and chopsticks are on sale along with contemporary items such as mobile-phone knick-knacks, figurines and jewellery.

If you've worked up an appetite and are feeling brave, **Yakiya** (3-11-15 Yanaka, Taito-ku; map D5) is a well-liked spot serving fried squid on a cracker; its popularity is attested to by the persisting queue of eager customers.

Another nearby go-to spot for what the Japanese call 'B-grade gourmet' – essentially non-mainstream food that has more personality – is **Shipoya** (3-11-12

Yanaka, Taito-ku; map D5), or 'tail shop'. Here you can choose from a dozen varieties of pan-fried donuts in shapes inspired by cats' tails.

At candy-maker **Amezaiku Yoshihara** (1-23-5 Sendagi, Bunkyo-ku; map C5), you can watch the proprietor shape a piece of sweet from sugar syrup into one of a myriad of creatures of your own choosing. Utilising only fingers and scissors, it's a craft that was once a popular form of entertainment for Japanese children.

Gorge on games and anime, then drink robot-themed coffee at Gundam Café

As Japan's economy matured, Akihabara upgraded itself from a postwar hub for black marketeers and electronics tinkerers to the nation's retail centre for games, manga and anime. A true devotee could spend days wandering its endless aisles of media consumption.

Mandarake is a temple of anime, manga and collectibles ranging from Godzilla-genre monster movies to TV action figures like Ultraman, characters such as Hello Kitty, and trains, planes and cars. Begin your journey at the top and work your way down its eight floors.

With an ever-growing number of female fans for anime, Japan's biggest shopping chain for anime goods, Animate, got ahead of the curve and opened **Animate Akiba Girls Station**. The shop offers seven girl-friendly floors of anime, audiovisual goods and games, as well as a level for self-published manga called *doujinshi*, and *yaoi* ('boys' love') materials (fans – you know who you are).

Older *otaku* ('fanboys') will get a kick out of **Super Potato**, a shop dedicated to retro Japanese gaming systems and software. With a vast array of used game cartridges, discs and accessories, this is the place to pick up that vintage Nintendo you've been lusting after.

Now that your arms are weighed down with booty, it's time to recharge at the futuristic **Gundam Café**. Themed around the *Mobile Suit Gundam* animation series about giant robot suits steered by humans, the shop features Gundam-themed lattés, cakes and parfaits, and a shop where you can pick up novelty goods.

Mandarake; 3-11-12 Sotokanda, Chiyoda-ku; tel: 3252-7007; https://earth. mandarake.co.jp/shop/cmp; daily 10am–10.30pm; map D1

Animate Akiba Girls Station; 1-2-13, Sotokanda, Chiyoda-ku; tel: 3526-3977; daily 10am–9pm; map D1

Super Potato; 3F-5F, 1-11-2 Sotokanda, Chiyoda-ku; tel: 5289-9933; daily 11am–10pm; map D1

Gundam Café; 1-1 Kanda Hanaokacho, Chiyoda-ku; tel: 3251-0078; http://g-cafe. jp/en; daily 10am–10.30pm; map E1

Get lost in a rowdy former black market, Ameyoko

While much of Tokyo's gritty post-war legacy has been buried under the Japanese economic miracle, **Ameyoko** offers a taste of when times were tough and folks chis-elled their survival from a city bru-talised by World War II. The street market is far tamer than when it was a haunt for gangsters in the Occupation period, but it still evokes a rough-and-tumble past in a way only a few areas of the capital do.

One theory holds that the 'Ame' in Ameyoko stands for America (*yoko* means 'next to'). US soldiers came to this area near Ueno Sta-tion to hawk supplies to whole-salers, who then marked it up and sold it on to the locals. A second theory says that 'Ame', a Japanese type of sweet, gave the area its name because of its many sweets shops. Either way, apparently sens-ing opportunity, Ameyoko attracted *yakuza* (Japanese gangsters) look-ing to move in on the action, and the area became a hotbed of crime.

In addition to sweet shops selling Japanese confectionary like *anpan* (bean buns), these days you'll find an assortment of army surplus stores, shops selling American-style jeans and T-shirts (likely made in China), jewellers, watch sellers, fish shops, restaurants and more. Shop owners call out to pas-sersby to come in and sample their wares, touting the latest in-stock items and deals.

One recommendation for your sweet tooth is **Chanokiminoen**, a spot that specialises in *matcha* (green tea) soft-serve ice cream. Located smack in the middle of Ameyoko, Chanokiminoen is a tea seller that developed its own approach to ice cream, swirling *matcha* and vanilla together in an unbeatable combination.

Ameyoko market; 4-9-14 Ueno, Taito-ku; www.ameyoko.net; daily 10am–8pm; map E3
Chanokiminoen; 4-9-13 Ueno, Taito-ku; tel: 3342-0506; daily 10am–10pm; map E3

Learn about Japan's flora and fauna at the National Museum of Nature and Science

Befitting its role as the capital of one of the world's great science nations, Tokyo has not one but three science museums. Among them, the **National Museum of Nature and Science** is the elder statesman.

Established in a dignified building in the northeast corner of Ueno Park in 1877, the museum boasts one of the deepest histories of any in Japan. It's the country's only nationally administered comprehensive science museum, and a main institute for research in natural history, science and technology.

Among the over four million specimens preserved in the museum's collection is a huge skeleton of a Futabasaurus, a terrifying variety of archaic marine reptile found in Fukushima Prefecture in 1968. The skeleton is part of an exhibition showing how the Japanese islands underwent rapid fluctuations due to crustal movements, leading to the formation of complex geological structures and diverse forms of life.

Another room is devoted to Japanese people and nature. Here you'll learn how, around 40,000 years ago, Japanese people's ancestors encountered a land rich in forests and oceans at the eastern edge of Asia, interacting with the environment through the invention of pottery, the cultivation of plants and other techniques.

Learn too about the recent technological and scientific achievements of Japan. Discover the history of industrial technology in the country and peruse famous items like a Mitsubishi Zero Fighter. New to the museum is the excellent 'Global Environment Detector', which shows fluctuating images and data on Earth in semi-real-time.

The National Museum of Nature and Science has made great strides in recent years, and in advance of the Tokyo 2020 Olympics is working to offer even better signage and guided tours for English-speaking visitors.

National Museum of Nature and Science; 7-20 Uenokoen, Taito-ku; tel: 5777-8600; www.kahaku.go.jp; Tue–Sun 9am–5pm; map E3

Step back in time to old Tokyo at the Shitamachi Museum

'Shitamachi' is a term you hear fairly frequently in regards to Japanese culture. Meaning roughly 'low city', it refers to the flatlands east of the Palace and close to the Sumida River where artisans and merchants lived – folks who developed much of the arts, crafts and commercial culture we associate with Tokyo today. Much of Shitamachi was destroyed in the 1923 Great Kanto Earthquake and the 1945 firebombing, but its lifestyles have been preserved at the charming **Shitamachi Museum**.

Located on Shinobazu Pond in Ueno Park, the museum contains a full-size replica of the home of a merchant (dealing in Japanese-style wooden clogs called *geta*). In front are parked an old-fashioned rickshaw and hand-pulled cart. A row of wooden tenement house apartments called *nagaya* demonstrates the cramped quarters in which residents lived in bygone days. Tableaux include a mother and daughter selling sweets in a small shop next to their living quarters, and a coppersmith labouring and selling wares at his home.

On the second floor, you'll find a number of pre-electric household objects that were actually used by the original owners during the Taisho period (1912–1926).

Shitamachi Museum; 2-1 Ueno-koen, Taito-ku; tel: 3823-7451; www.taitocity.net/zaidan/shitamachi; Tue–Sun 9.30am–4.30pm; map E3

ASAKUSA AND EAST TOKYO

Asakusa and East Tokyo

ARAKAWA-KU

Nippori

YANAKA-REIEN

Sendagi

Zuirin-ji

Uguisudani

Nezu-jinja   Gyokurin-ji

Tokyo Kokuritsu
Hakubutsukan
(Tokyo National Museum)

Nezu

Kokuritsu Kahaku Hakubutsukan
(National Museum of Nature and Science)

BUNKYO-KU

Kokuritsu Seiyo Bijutsukan
(National Museum of Western Art)

Todaimae

TAITO-KU

UENO-KŌEN

Ueno

KAMATA
Hakensha

Tokyo Daigaku
(Tokyo University)

Shinobazu
Pond

Ueno

Asakusa-dōri

Taikoku
(Drum Muse)

Keiseiueno

Maizuru

Okuda
Shouten

Kasuga

Hongo-
sanchōme

Ueno-okachimachi

Inarichō

Nakaokachi-
machi

Tawaramac

Korakuen

Kasuga-dōri

Ueno-hirokōji

Shinokachimachi

Kasuga-dōri

Kokusai-dōri

Asakusa Toei
Theatre

Hanayashiki
Amusement Park

Kuramae

Hisago-dōri

Asakusa
-jinja

Kuramaebashi-dōri

Sensō-ji

ASAKUSA

Gojuno-tō
(Five Storey
Pagoda)

Amuse
Museum

Niten-mon

Hōzō-mon
(Treasury Gate)

HANA-
KAWADO

Asakusa-
bashi

Ryogoku Kok
(Ryogoku S

Asakusabashi

Rokku Broadway

Asakusa
Engei Hall

ROX

Benten-dō

Kanda

Ry
Tomoe
Chanko M

Denbo-in

Samurai Training
Experience

Bakurochō

Momonjiy

Jakotsu-yu

ROX DOME

Denboin-dōri

Asakusa
Public Hall

Umamichi-dōri

Kannon-dōri

Higashi-
nihombashi

Tobū-
Asakusa

Bakuro-
yokoyama

Susihaya-dōri

Orange-dōri

Chiyoko-dōri

Nakamise-dōri

SUMIDA-
KŌEN

Hamachō

NIHONBASH
HAMACHO PA

Kaminarimon-dōri

Matsuya
Dept Store

Edo-dōri

Asakusa

Ningyōchō

Arashi
Beya

KAMINARIMON

Kaminari-mon
(Thunder Gate)

Waterbus
Station

Sumida

Suitengumae

Azuma-bashi

Shin-ōhashi-dōri

100 m

100 yds

Gallery éf

Fukagawa

Arashio Beya **D2**
Drum Museum **D4**
Edo-Tokyo Museum **E2**
Hanayashiki Amusement Park **A/B3**
KAMATA Hakensha **D4**
Maizuru **D4**
Momonjiya **D2**
Museum of Contemporary Art, Tokyo **F1**
Okuda Shouten **D4**
Ryogoku Sumo Hall **D2**
Samurai Training Experience **B2**
Sensō-ji **B3**
Tokyo Skytree **F3**
Tomoegata Chanko Nabe **D2**

Train in the art of samurai sword fighting and snatch a selfie in full regalia

With the surge in overseas tourism has come a profusion of firms offering experiences targeting foreigners with an interest in Japanese culture – from cooking to flower arranging. Atop many visitors' list is a fascination with Japan's tradition of samurai sword fighting, and there's now a company that offers a full samurai training experience.

Sword master Ukon Takafuji runs **Samurai Training Experience** out of a studio in the central Asakusa district, just a stone's throw from the hallowed Senso-ji (see page 139). An hour-long course in ken-

Japanese swordsmanship

The renowned *katana* (Japanese sword) was first created in the 8th century. The three leading schools of swordsmanship arose during the Muromachi era (c.14–16th centuries), a period known for long intervals of conflict.

jutsu – the samurai art of swordsmanship – will cost you ¥7,000.

Takafuji and his assistants will first ask you to take your shoes off and change into traditional costume. You will then be walked through the essential paces of Japanese swordsmanship, including overhead slices and defensive moves. Of key importance are the traditional greetings, vocalisations and bowings that accompany *kenjutsu* practice.

The session culminates in a rehearsed battle, followed by still poses with your blade, all of which will be documented for posterity by Takafuji's helpful retinue. While there's only so much you can learn in an hour, it's good fun and guaranteed to bring out the inner child warrior in anyone.

Samurai Training Experience; 2F, 1-36-8 Asakusa, Taito-ku; tel: 5770-5131; www.tokyo-samurai.com/experience; map B2

Tour Tokyo's oldest temple, Senso-ji, and snag some knick-knacks for friends back home

The Asakusa area is the heart of Tokyo's historic downtown district, and **Senso-ji** is its pulse. The temple has attracted pilgrims for a thousand years and continues to act as a lively confluence of worship and commercial hubbub.

Legend holds that a statue of the Buddhist goddess of mercy, Kannon, was found in the nearby Sumida River in 628 by two fisherman. Their village head placed the statue in a small shrine he built in Asakusa, and a temple has existed there ever since – making it Tokyo's oldest. With more than 30 million annual visitors, it's also reportedly the world's most visited spiritual site.

Senso-ji is approached via the imposing **Thunder Gate** (Kaminari-mon). The structure features a giant *chochin* – a lantern – painted in vibrant black, white and red to suggest thunderclouds.

Passing through the gate, you'll find yourself in the **Nakamise-dori**, a long pedestrian lane lined with souvenir shops. The commercial clutter is the latest iteration of a tradition of merchants gathering to attend to pilgrims' needs, a common feature of temples throughout Asia.

The 820ft (250-metre) approach to the shrine contains about

80 shops. Choose from among traditional textiles, footwear, dolls and Buddhist scrolls, or pick up a Godzilla or Hello Kitty-themed accessory for your mobile. If you're hungry, try out a classic Tokyo confection like *ningyoyaki* ('doll cake') or *kaminari-okoshi* (sweet rice crackers).

Senso-ji; 2-3-1 Asakusa, Taito-ku; tel: 3842-0181; www.senso-ji.jp; daily 6am–5pm; map B3

Brave the rickety rides of Hanayashiki, Japan's oldest amusement park

Hanayashiki is like New York's Coney Island: people visit not for the latest high-tech rollercoasters, but for a charmingly retro experience, which offers a glimpse of the amusement-park world before the likes of Disneyland. Founded in 1853 as a flower park, Hanayashiki (meaning 'flower estate') is particularly worthwhile if you're with kids and not planning the trek to Tokyo Disney Resort.

Enter at the main gate just a short walk from Asakusa Station. The park manages to squeeze a lot of atmosphere and rides into its limited space. Among its attractions are a Thriller Car, Ferris wheel, a vertical drop called Space Shot and a relatively tame haunted house. The rollercoaster offers plenty of thrills – for the little ones anyway – and claims to be the oldest steel-track coaster in Japan, built in 1953.

Don't miss the Bee Tower, which you ascend in gondolas and from which you can enjoy panoramic views of Asakusa and the Sumida River area. There are also offbeat, Japan-specific attractions like a tiny pond where you can fish for baby lobster with a miniature fishing rod, or classes in which can learn about the tea ceremony, don a kimono or experience being a ninja for an hour.

Hanayashiki; Asakusa 2-28-1, Taito-ku; tel: 3842-8780; http://hanayashiki.net/e; daily 10am–6pm; map A/B3

Muse on the meaning of art at the Museum of Contemporary Art, Tokyo

Though somewhat eclipsed by the centrally located Mori Art Museum, the **Museum of Contemporary Art, Tokyo (MOT)** remains a must-see for fans of current Japanese art. Takahiko Yanagisawa's imposing rectilinear building juts out from the surrounding low-rise, old-school Kiba neighbourhood, housing a substantial collection of post-war art, both Japanese and international. Please note that the MOT is closed until 2018 for a major renovation.

Opened in 1995 next to Kiba Park, the museum ushers visitors into Yanagisawa's giant maw of a lobby, an impressive welcome into three floors (43,000 sq ft/4,000 sq metres) of galleries devoted to temporary exhibitions and two further floors (32,300 sq ft/3,000 sq metres) for 'MOT Collection' exhibitions, making it the largest contemporary art museum in the country.

Among the MOT's collections are significant pieces by domestic artists, ranging from Chimei Hamada's meditation on the injustices of contemporary society, *Deranged Man*, to Makoto Aida's disturbing 'War Picture Returns' series. Major exhibitions have also been devoted to the playful, conceptual provocations of Yoko Ono (best known as the wife of Beatle John Lennon) that reveal the turbid Tokyo scene in the 1950s, 60s and 70s, and how Ono's activities connected Japan to art currents underway in Europe and the United States.

Top off your visit with a wander outside in the museum's serene grounds and/or lunch at the pleasant café.

Museum of Contemporary Art, Tokyo (Tokyo-to Gendai Bijutsu-kan); 4-1-1 Miyoshi, Koto-ku; tel: 5245-4111; www.mot-art-museum.jp; map F1

Feel the pulse of Japan at the Drum Museum

From the rowdiest traditional neighbourhood festival to the most serene court music, drums are essential to Japanese performing arts. If you're interested in Japanese culture or are simply a percussion fan, an hour spent in Asakusa's **Drum Museum** (Taikokan) makes for a highly pleasurable and educational experience.

The museum is run by and located above **Miyamoto Unosuke Co.**, a maker of *taiko* (drums) and festival instruments since 1861. Take the lift up to the fourth floor and enter a kingdom of percussion, both Japanese and from around the world.

Taiko are featured in *Gagaku* court music and traditional *Noh* and *Kabuki* theatre, but their widest use is in traditional festivals called *matsuri*. Some *matsuri* are religious and centre around Buddhist temples or Shinto shrines, while others commemorate a military victory or local lord. Bon Odori is a typical summer festival in which neighbourhood *taiko* groups provide the soundtrack for dancing, which is meant to summon ancestral spirits. In recent years, professional groups – like Kodo – have elevated Japanese drums to an art form, touring the world with athletic displays that draw rapturous audiences.

At Taikokan you can learn about the different types of *taiko*. Miyamoto's craftsmen spend years curing wood and tanning leather to make the larger instruments that can cost tens of thousands of pounds. English signs explain the roots and purpose of each drum, and better still, visitors are invited to bang away on the instruments. On the first floor you can shop for *bachi* (drum sticks), bells or festival clothing as a keepsake of your trip.

Drum Museum (Taikokan); 2-1-1 Nishiasakusa, Taito-ku; tel: 3844-2141; www.miyamoto-unosuke.co.jp; Wed–Sun 10am–5pm; map D4

Navigate a historic Tokyo waterway on a *yakatabune* dining boat

With its numerous rivers and expansive waterfront, Tokyo offers a number of cruising possibilities. Among the options, the *yakatabune* are the only boats that offer a traditional Japanese *omotenashi* (hospitality) experience. Situate yourself on *tatami* (woven straw) mats, get tipsy and watch the city glide by as you dine on gourmet cuisine.

Yakatabune boats are built the old-fashioned way, with low profiles, protruding *miyoshi* bows and lanterns under the roof. It's believed *yakatabune* were developed by aristocrats in medieval times, they reached their apex in the 17th and 18th centuries, when cruises on the Sumida River became popular among wealthy merchants and elite samurai.

In two to three-hour programmes, passengers are seated on *tatami* mats and served traditional multi-course *(kaiseki)* menus that often feature several appetisers, sashimi, tempura, rice, soup and a dessert.

Most of the operators also offer all-you-can-drink selections of beer, sake, plum brandy and the like.

Tours generally navigate the Sumida River, offering spectacular views of the Tokyo Skytree (see page 144) reflected in the waters, before heading out into Tokyo Bay where the Rainbow Bridge sits picturesquely against the modern cityscape. Night-time tours are recommended for best viewing. As the sake soaks in and you and your fellow riders enjoy the views together, conversation is bound to begin and you may leave with some new friends.

Thirty-five *yakatabune* operators offer varying experiences from several different departure points. They generally cost about ¥10,000 for the dinner cruise. You can make a reservation via the **Tokyo Yakatabune Association** website.

Tokyo Yakatabune Association;
www.yakatabune-kumiai.jp/en

Survey Japan's capital from Tokyo Skytree, the world's tallest tower

Boasting observation decks at 1,150ft and 1,475ft (350 and 450 metres), **Tokyo Skytree** isn't for those with a fear of heights. The neo-futuristic broadcasting tower has become a sightseeing landmark since its completion in 2012, and for engineering geeks and those who simply love a good view however, a visit is imperative.

The Skytree was designed by Nikken Sekkei with a triangular base tapering to a conical top. It attained its full height of 2,080ft (634 metres) in 2011, becoming the tallest tower on the planet and second tallest structure after the Burj Khalifa in Dubai.

If you're already in Asakusa, you can walk here, enjoying fantastic views along the way as you cross the Sumida River. Alternatively, you can access the tower from Tokyo Skytree or Oshiage stations. At the base of the tower is a large mall where you can eat before or after your visit.

Purchase your tickets at the fourth-floor ticket counter. For ¥2,060 you can ascend to the 1,150ft (350-metre), 3000-capacity Tembo Deck. An extra ¥1,030 gets you to the smaller, 1,475ft (450-metre) Tembo Galleria, which features a wrap-around, ascending hallway. If time is limited and lines are long, Fast Skytree Tickets can be had for ¥3,000 and ¥4,000.

Visit at the end of the day if you can to enjoy a leisurely view of the sun setting behind Mount Fuji, as the Tokyo nightscape comes alive in a twinkling display of fathomless urban sprawl.

Tokyo Skytree; 1-1-2 Oshiage, Sumida-ku; tel: 0570-550-634; www.tokyo-skytree.jp; daily 8am–10pm; map F3

Free views

Those on a shoestring budget should head to the **Tokyo Metropolitan Government Building** in Shinjuku, which has a free observation deck at 663ft (202 metres).

Discover the past – and present – of Japan's capital at the Edo-Tokyo Museum

Fires, earthquakes and war have sadly erased most of Tokyo's physical past, but successful efforts have been made to preserve and reconstruct it in the vast spaces of the **Edo-Tokyo Museum** in Ryogoku. A few hours spent learning about this ever-evolving megalopolis is time well spent. Be aware, however, that the Edo-Tokyo Museum will be closed for renovation from 1 October 2017 to 31 March 2018.

The Edo-Tokyo Museum occupies a giant concrete structure that hovers above its surroundings on enormous pillars. The museum sits next to the Ryogoku Sumo Hall and was designed by Kiyonori Kikutake, who modelled it on an old elevated storehouse.

Enter the permanent exhibition space and find a life-size replica of the Nihonbashi Bridge leading into Edo (Tokyo's name before it became the capital) and scale models of buildings from the Edo, Meiji and Showa periods. Carefully prepared side exhibitions showcase original objects, taking visitors on a journey through the 400-year history of Edo-Tokyo since Tokugawa Ieyasu entered Edo. Rare photo and film footage also documents tragic events including the Great Kato Earthquake that killed more than 100,000 in 1923 and the firebombing that took a similar number of lives in 1945.

In addition to the permanent collection, the museum holds intriguing exhibitions at the first-floor gallery several times a year, as well as other events including lectures and workshops on the history and culture of Edo-Tokyo.

Edo-Tokyo Museum (Edo-Tokyo Hakubutsukan); 1-4-1 Yokoami, Sumida-ku; tel: 3626-9974; www.edo-tokyo-museum. or.jp, Tue–Sun 9.30am–5.30pm; map E2

Watch sumo giants clash at the Ryogoku Kokugikan, or in morning practice at a sumo stable

Salt is ritually tossed into the ring, the referee cries out and two sumo leviathans hurl 24-plus stone of muscle and sinew against each other in a contest decided in nail-biting seconds. There are few experiences as quintessentially Japanese as sumo, a practice that is as much religious rite as athletic competition.

Should you be in Tokyo during January, May or September, the opportunity exists to attend a *basho* (tournament). Six 15-day *basho* are held across Japan in professional sumo, three of them in Tokyo. If you are unable to make one, then it is also possible to visit a training stable and observe wrestlers labour through their morning routines.

Basho in Tokyo are held at the **Ryogoku Sumo Hall** (Ryogoku Kokugikan), just across the Sumida River from Asakusa. The 13,000-seat building was opened in 1985, replacing previous sumo arenas on the site. (It will also host boxing during the 2020 Tokyo Olympics.)

Booking a ticket online has become simple, with a number of operators (including the Kokugikan's website itself) offering English interfaces and the option of joining an English guided tour. Tickets range from ¥3,800 for high-up arena seats to ¥38,000 for ringside,

tatami-style box seats, where you will literally be able to smell the sweat of the *rikishi* (wrestlers).

Arrive early and see robed *rikishi* walking to the Kokugikan for the day's bouts, then peruse the **Sumo Museum**, which displays *nishiki-e* woodblock prints, *banzuke* (tournament record books) and *kesho-mawashi* (the belts worn for ceremony by top-ranked *rikishi*).

Bottom-ranked *rikishi* kick off the action at 9am, followed by the leading wrestlers in the afternoon. Locals often don't arrive until later in the day, when bouts between the top-ranked *sekiwake* and *ozeki* sumo divisions, and finally the grand champion *yokozuna*, take place. As the action heats up, chants become louder. A particularly heated match may climax with fans throwing cushions into the ring to express anger at an underperforming *rikishi*.

If you're unable to see a tournament but are still hankering to see *rikishi* up close, visit morning practice at a sumo *beya* (stable). Most *beya*, which also provide living quarters for wrestlers, are clustered in and around Ryogoku.

With a little advance planning, it's possible to watch sessions, which begin around 5am and last for three or four hours. While some *beya* don't welcome viewers, several are more than happy to accommodate them. **Arashio Beya** has an English website where you can find information on how to visit, but due to its popularity tourists are now asked to watch through large windows.

Hakkuku Beya, **Kasugano Beya** and **Kokonoe Beya** are also known to receive visitors, who will be asked to sit quiet and motionless on cushions so as not to distract the *rikishi*. If you wish to visit one of these *beya*, it's best to ask the Japanese receptionist at your hotel to call a day ahead and make reservations.

Finish up your sumo experience with a bowl of the *rikishi*'s favourite *chanko nabe* (a weight-gain stew). **Tomoegata Chanko Nabe** is known to serve one of the best versions of this aromatic blend of vegetables, meat and tofu.

Ryogoku Sumo Hall (Ryogoku Kokugikan); 1-3-28 Yokoami, Sumida-ku; tel: 3623-5111; www.sumo.or.jp/En; map D2
Arashio Beya; 2-47-2, Hama-cho Nihonbashi, Chuo-ku; tel: 3666-7646; www.arashio.net/tour_e.html; map D2
Tomoegata Chanko Nabe; 2-17-6 Ryogoku, Sumida-ku; tel: 3632-5600; tomoegata.com; Mon–Fri 11.30am–2pm and 5–11pm, Sat–Sun 11.30am–2pm and 4.30–11pm, June–Aug closed Mon; map D2

Marvel at the plastic-display food and kitchenware of Kappabashi

Tsukiji tops the list for foodies heading to Japan, but the plastic food displays and endless kitchenware on **Kappabashi** comprise a veritable playground for anyone who likes to cook. If you're in Asakusa or Ueno, a stroll down Kappabashi Dougu (meaning 'tool thoroughfare') is a rewarding way to spend an hour – you may even come away with some incredibly well-crafted kitchen goods.

Merchants first came to the Kappabashi area a century ago, selling old kitchenware. Today, sellers hawk everything from baking equipment to tableware, *noren* (shop curtains) and bamboo ware, and of course the famous 'fake' food samples. With more than 170 shops, Kappabashi Dougu is Japan's largest street devoted to the kitchen.

Plastic food displays spread in Japan's restaurants in the late 1920s to make it easy for custom-ers to order without menus, which were rare at that time. The skilled craftsmen at shops like **Maizuru** (1-5-17 Nishiasakusa, Taito-ku; tel: 3843-1686; map D4) still produce plastic food items by hand. Two outlets in Kappabashi sell items – ranging from sushi to cold beer – available in miniature magnet size for your fridge back home.

Instantly recognisable by its large sign with a vertical blade, knife-specialist **KAMATA Hakensha** (2-12-6 Matsugaya, Taito-ku; tel: 3841-4205; http://kap-kam.com; map D4) is another must-see. Tokyo's sushi chefs come here in search of the perfect blade, trusting KAMATA's selection of the sharpest edges from around Japan. A set of the wood-handled knives called *wabocho* makes a great souvenir for your family and friends.

If you're into cooking, **Okuda Shouten** (1-5-10 Nishiasakusa, Taito-ku; tel: 3844-4511; map D4) offers a wide range of bamboo implements used in the Japanese kitchen. Choose from among strainers, steamers, bamboo baskets for soba, chopsticks, *handai* (used for making sushi rice), bento boxes and soup bowls. Most shops in Kappabashi are open Monday to Friday from 9am to 5pm.

Dine on wild boar or venison _sukiyaki_ at centuries-old Momonjiya

It's not widely known, but guns are legal in Japan and the country has a long tradition of game hunting Notwithstanding Buddhist prohibitions against eating meat, **Momonjiya**, not far from the Tokyo Skytree and Sumida River, has been serving wild boar, bear and venison since 1718. The name itself is an archaic word for a shop that sells game.

Momonjiya is instantly recognisable by the large boar that adorns the entrance, and the _tatami_ (straw mat) flooring and low tables inside suit the restaurant's historic air. Choose from among different _nabe_ (hot pot) dishes that are prepared either _shabu-shabu_-style with thinly sliced meat in boiling water with dipping sauces, or in _sukiyaki_ fashion, heavily flavoured with salty soy sauce and sweet mirin rice wine. Momonjiya prides itself on the top quality of its meat: its low fat wild boar, marbled bear steak and fine-grained venison are carefully selected by experienced traders. The meat will be served to you raw – along with a variety of fresh vegetables – for you to simmer in the hot pot at your table. The longer it's boiled, the more flavourful the meat becomes.

With an English menu and English-speaking staff, the whole affair is as easy as it is delicious.

Animal attacks

As Japan's countryside depopulates, rural villages are experiencing a surge in wild boar and bear attacks.

Momonjiya; 1-10-2 Ryogoku, Sumida-ku; tel: 3469-3543; Mon–Sat 5–9pm; map D2

BEYOND THE CITY CENTRE

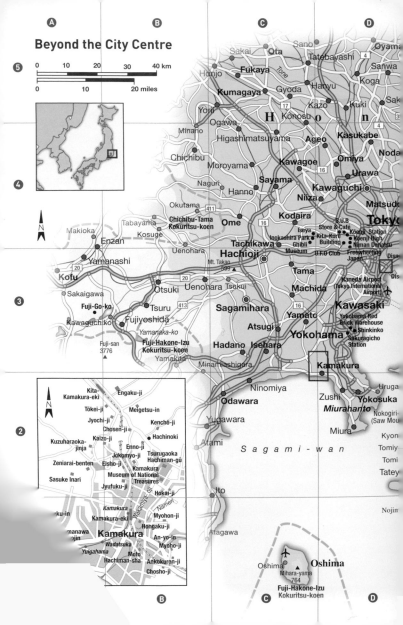

Cross Rainbow Bridge to futuristic Odaiba and bathe in hot springs at Ooedo Onsen Monogatari

Odaiba, a giant artificial island in Tokyo Bay named for a cannon emplacement, best embodies the *Blade Runner* vision of Japan's capital. Vast architectural hulks from the future are scattered across a blank canvas of newly created land.

Access Odaiba via the cutting-edge Yurikamome line or the new underground Rinkai line. Better yet, take in stunning views of the cityscape across the water by navigating your way across the Rainbow Bridge. From Shibaura-Futo Station, a walkway leads across the 3,012ft (918-metre) suspension bridge. Crossing it takes 30–40 minutes.

Back on firm ground, there are a number of museums and entertainment and shopping destinations to choose from. (One of the best museums is the National Museum of Emerging Science and Innovation – see page 165.)

DECKS Tokyo Beach (1-6-1 Daiba, Minato-ku; tel: 3599-6500; www.odaiba-decks.com; map G1) is a shopping and amusement complex that includes the state-of-art arcade **Joypolis** (http://tokyo-joypolis.com) and plenty of places to eat. More trendy shops, Sony's **ExploraScience** museum (www.sonyexplorascience.jp) and a multiplex cinema can be found next door at **Aqua City** (1-7-1 Daiba, Minato-ku; tel: 3599-4700; www.aquacity.jp; map G1).

From both locations you can't fail to notice the astonishing Kenzo Tange-designed **Fuji TV Building**, consisting of two blocks connected by girder-like sky corridors and a giant titanium-panelled sphere.

On the far side of Fuji TV, you'll find **DiverCity Tokyo Plaza** (1-1-10 Aomi, Koto-ku; tel: 6380-7800; www.divercity-tokyo.com; map G1), another vast shopping and recreational complex. The most notable attraction here is **Round 1 Stadium** (www.round1.co.jp/shop/tenpo/tokyo-divercity.html), one of the largest entertainment centres in Tokyo, where you can go bowling, fine tune those karaoke skills and play games ranging from air hockey to table tennis, pool to darts. For the admission fee you can use everything.

Don't forget to check out **Gundam Base Tokyo** (www.gundam-base.net/en), an all-new shopping and entertainment centre – also in DiverCity – devoted to the beloved TV series. It has a 'Gunpla' (Gundam plastic model) builders' room and 'Bandai Hobby Center' illuminating the Gunpla manufacturing process.

Now it's time to breathe a sigh of relief and sink into the steamy waters of the extraordinary **Ooedo Onsen Monogatari** (2-6-3 Aomi, Koto-ku; tel: 5500-1126; www.ooedoonsen.jp; map G1), a recently constructed but traditional hot spring with outdoor and indoor tubs, a sand bath, saunas and foot-massage baths.

City defences

The name Odaiba comes from the cannon emplacements built in Tokyo Bay in 1853 to defend the city against any attack by American Commodore Perry's Black Ships. The remnants of two cannons can still be seen today.

Source some only-in-Japan swag at Tokyo Disneyland and DisneySea

There are many good reasons to visit **Tokyo Disney Resort**. Firstly, it hosts the world's only **DisneySea**, an adult-oriented, nautically themed park with rides you won't find anywhere else. Secondly, you can pick up charming Japanese goodies to impress the folks back home. Thirdly, the whole Tokyo Disney Resort complex is less than an hour from the town centre, accessible via the themed Disney Resort-line monorail.

Opened in 2001, DisneySea is the 9th of 11 Disney parks. Inside, you'll find a host of attractions that offer more thrills than the usual Disneyland ride. Toy Story Mania is a highlight, offering a carnival world and the chance to 'toss' items like bananas at on-screen targets, while 20,000 Leagues Under the Sea is a rip-roaring Jules Verne-inspired plunge through the deep. DisneySea's resident volcano, Mount Prometheus, erupts spectacularly every few hours.

Japan's manufacturers have spared no effort when it comes to devising unique, only-in-Japan swag for the local Disney machine. Many of the best items are found in the kitchenware section at the Home Store at the World Bazaar. Choose from traditional blue-on-white glazed ramen bowls and plates, or Mickey-themed chopsticks.

Turning to food itself, you'll find unbearably cute creations such as the *ukiwaman* (swim float-shaped buns) at DisneySea's Port Discovery, and Little Green Men rice-cake buns from *Toy Story* at the Mediterranean Harbor. You'll also come across unique adaptations of popcorn, such as milk-tea popcorn available at DisneySea's American Waterfront, and at **Tokyo Disneyland**, flavours including curry and soy sauce and butter.

Both parks are crowded day and night, year-round. Your best bet for a quieter experience is a cold and rainy weekday.

Tokyo Disney Resort (Tokyo Disneyland and Tokyo DisneySea); 1-1 Maihama, Urayasu; tel: 045-330-5211; www.tokyo disneyresort.jp; map D3

Visit anime legend Hayao Miyazaki's Ghibli Museum and relax in Inokashira Park

In the quiet suburb of Mitaka in western Tokyo is a shrine to anime auteur Hayao Miyazaki that fans won't want to miss. The **Ghibli Museum** celebrates the animated films of Miyazaki's Studio Ghibli, including *Spirited Away* and *Howl's Moving Castle*, and reveals Miyazaki's working process. Keep in mind before you go that tickets must be reserved in advance through the museum's website.

The Ghibli Museum is housed in a fanciful building on the edge of **Inokashira Park**, and lies within walking distance of both Mitaka and Kichijoji stations. The first installation you'll notice is a giant 'Cat Bus', straight out of *My Neighbor Totoro*. The museum apparently wanted to make a bus-sized cat, but it wouldn't fit inside. The plush, grinning animal is limited to kids aged 12 and under – who can climb on it and stroke its fluffy fur – and who may have to be prised off when it's time to leave.

Another permanent feature is the revealing '*Ponyo on the Cliff by the Sea*' exhibition, which provides interesting insights into Miyazaki's thoughts and methods. The museum also offers thought-provoking temporary exhibitions.

A walk through leafy Inokashira Park makes the perfect cap to a visit to the Ghibli Museum. Meander your way through the park, perhaps even enjoying a boat ride on the pond along the way, to Kichijoji on the far side. The area is a long-time student haunt and is famed for its many bars, cafés, restaurants and clubs.

Next to the park is **Iseya**, a legendary *yakitori* (chicken skewers) restaurant looking out on the trees. Order a *nama biru* (draft beer), some *tsukune* (chicken balls) with *tare* (sweet soy sauce) or *shio* (salt) seasoning and discuss the museum's highlights.

Ghibli Museum (Bijutsukan); 1-1-83 Simorenjaku, Mitaka-shi; www.ghibli-museum.jp; daily 10am–6pm; map C4
Iseya; 1-15-8 Kichijoji Minamicho, Musashino-shi; tel: 0422-43-2806; kichijoji-iseya.jp; noon–10pm; map C4

Spend an afternoon touring the stately shrines and giant Buddhas of Kamakura

If you can't make it to Kyoto, there's another ancient capital chock-a-block with historic temples, mossy gardens and intriguing craft shops. **Kamakura** was the shogun's hub between 1192 and 1333, but is now a leafy suburb where giant Buddhas share space with up-market residences and chic restaurants.

Begin at Kita-Kamakura Station, from where it's only a two-minute walk to a cluster of temples. Embraced by ancient cedars, **Engaku-ji** (Yamanouchi 409, Kamakura-shi; tel: 0467-220 478; www.engakuji.or.jp; map B2) is a major temple complex that was founded in 1282 to honour the soldiers who were killed during Kublai Khan's failed invasion. Planned according to Zen principles, the main buildings and numerous temples possess an austere beauty, softened by foliage, shrubbery and a pond. The Chinese-style **Shari-den**, one of the finest buildings here, is said to contain a tooth of the Buddha.

Continue southeast until you reach **Tokei-ji** (1367 Yamanouchi, Kamakura-shi; tel: 0467-221 663; www.tokeiji.com; map A2), a 13th-century Buddhist temple that originally served as a nunnery. Known as the 'Divorce Temple', this was one of the few places where women could escape abusive husbands. Stroll through the flower-filled gardens to the temple's rear, where nuns lie buried beneath mossy headstones.

Follow the main Kamakura-kaido road across the tracks until you reach the grand entrance gate to **Kencho-ji** (8 Yamanouchi, Kamakura-shi; tel: 0467-220 981; www.kenchoji.com; map B2). Founded in 1253, this is one of Japan's oldest Zen temples. A grove of ancient junipers almost conceal the main **Buddha Hall**, which houses the bodhisattva Jizo, floating on a bed of lotuses. **Hojo**, the abbot's quarters and the finest wooden structure at Kencho-ji, looks onto an exquisite garden. Remove your shoes and walk along a balcony of timeworn wood to reach the garden. On leaving, you'll pass the Buddhist vegetarian restaurant **Hachinoki** (7 Yamanouchi, Kamakura; tel: 0467-23-3723; www.hachinoki.co.jp; map B2), a fitting stop for lunch.

Continue downhill towards Kamakura centre until you reach the **Tsurugaoka Hachiman-gu**, marked by a series of red *torii* gates. Since the 11th century this has been the guardian shrine for the Minamoto clan, founders of the Kamakura shogunate. The red-painted halls, souvenir stalls and flow of visitors make it one of the city's most colourful pilgrimage spots. A large gingko tree near the steps up to the shrine marks the spot where the third shogun was assassinated by his nephew in 1219.

Next, take the Enoden-line train which connects Kamakura and Enoshima, get off at Hase Station and walk to **Kotoku-in** (4-2-28 Hase, Kamakura-shi; tel: 0467-22-0703; www.kotoku-in.jp; map A1), which houses the Great Buddha (Daibutsu). Survivor of fires, typhoons and earthquakes, the 36ft (11-metre) Buddha is Japan's second-largest bronze statue. Cast in 1252, it suffered a series of catastrophes that culminated in a tidal wave that swept the building housing it away in 1495. These disasters were interpreted as a sign that the Buddha wished to remain outside, and the statue, exposed to the sun ever since, is now an oxidised, streaked green. For an extra sum you can clamber inside.

Zip through Tokyo's hidden byways by bike

It's a little-known fact that Tokyo is one of the world's best urban cycling spots. Despite a lack of bike infrastructure, the city's vast network of quiet backstreets makes it a real two-wheel charm. Join **Freewheeling Japan** for a tour through the intriguing neighbourhoods of western Tokyo and discover how Japanese people really live.

American expats Brad Bennett and Chad Feyen run Freewheeling out of an old home in Sasazuka, a few miles west of Shinjuku. Brad, Chad and their staff guide patrons through the Nakano and Shinjuku areas to trendy Meguro a few miles south, and as far west as the Tama River. You'll experience Tokyo from a local's point of view, disappearing into a maze of neighbourhood streets full of everyday life as you encounter highlights along the way.

The **Oomiya Hachiman** in Suginami ward, located next to the picturesque gardens of the Zenpukuji River, is a favourite stop. This grand shrine houses many *mikoshi* (festival floats) and has grounds for traditional archery practice.

The vibrant western Tokyo shopping districts of **Shimokitazawa** and **Tomigaya** are also on the circuit. Shimokitazawa was the centre of the 1960s counterculture and is now host to vintage clothing shops, funky cafés and boutiques, while Tomigaya is renowned for its endless shopping street.

Bennett and Feyen are well known to locals, and you'll likely find yourself stopping for an expert brew at places like the Little Nap coffee stand, whose staff know their coffee well and give an extra warm welcome to customers arriving by bicycle. Many spots are off the tourist map, unusual at a time when Japan has given up its secrets to the internet, and cameras are not permitted in some locations. Reservations can be made online.

Freewheeling Japan; 3-36-10 Sasazuka, Shibuya-ku; tel: 090-3450-5750; www.freewheeling.jp; map D4

Ascend temple-festooned Mount Takao and slurp a bowl of soba noodles

Just an hour from Shinjuku Station, the verdant trails, atmospheric temples and charming souvenir village of **Mount Takao** make it one of Tokyo's most popular day-trip destinations. Hike or take the funicular or lift to the summit, and if you're lucky you'll be rewarded with a sublime view across serried ranges to giant Mount Fuji itself.

As you depart the Keio line's Takaosanguchi Station you will see day trippers headed for the funicular and lift. If you choose to ride to the top, it takes six minutes and costs around ¥500 one way or ¥900 for the roundtrip. Better yet is to hike to the summit, a route that benefits from wooded paths, Buddhist temples and possible sightings of wild boars and monkeys.

There are seven climbing and hiking routes on Mount Takao. To reach the summit from the base takes about 1.5 hours. If pressed for time, speed up the process by taking the funicular halfway up and then climbing on foot toward the summit.

The most impressive of Takao's several religious institutions is **Yakuin**. Established in 744, Yakuin is one of the principal temples of the Shingon Buddhist sect. Takao is renowned as a centre of mountain asceticism (Shugendo) which demands strict discipline. Legend holds that the mountain is home to a Tengu, a fictitious being with supernatural powers believed to be a spirit of the mountain.

Choose a different route down for a variation in scenery, and dine at one of several soba noodle shops near the funicular station. The local speciality is *tororo* (yam) soba – grated mountain yams in a bowl of soba noodles.

Mount Takao (Takao-zan); Takao-machi, Hachioji; www.takaotozan.co.jp; map C3

Cruise counterculture capital Koenji and catch a gig at a 'live house'

Some of the satellite stations on Tokyo's hub-and-spokes transport network have morphed into hot-spots of their own. **Koenji**, just two stops from Shinjuku on the Chuo line, once enjoyed a reputation as a counterculture haven. These days, it's one of Tokyo's most vibrant youth-culture neighbourhoods, flooded with hipster cafés, book-shops, boutiques, record stores, bars and music venues called 'live

houses'. The secret is out – but don't let that stop you from whiling a day away in one of the capital's funnest areas.

A good blueprint for your outing is to alight at Koenji Station and then walk to Higashi Koenji Station on the Marunouchi line. This mile-long (1.5km) path will allow you to take in some of the zone's more interesting shops, sights and nightspots. Before you head south to Higashi Koenji, there are some unmissable spots near Koenji Station itself.

One of them is the **Kita-Kore Building** (3-4-11 Koenjikita, Suginami-ku; map D4), a shack-like structure that houses a collection of new and vintage clothing shops that define shabby-chic Tokyo style. The building includes works by designers like ilil, Dog and Hayatochiri, who are known for the remake fashion often featured in streetwear sections of Tokyo style websites.

Just north of the elevated tracks is the **S.U.B. Store & Café** (3-1-12 Koenjikita, Suginami-ku; map D4), a newish record and bookshop plus café. Run by a young Japanese-Indonesian couple, S.U.B. (which stands for 'Small-Unique-Bookstore') is a space where you can browse vintage punk LPs, leaf through a

selection of curated art and music books and dine on tasty Indonesian food. Night-times give way to hipster DJ events and even the occasional live-music gig.

Now that you're clothed and fed, head south of the station for a romp through Koenji's famous live houses. Closest to the station, **Koenji High** (4-30-1 Koenjiminami, Suginami-ku; map D4) hosts a blend of local and (occasionally) international rock acts.

Further south, on large boulevard One Kaido near Higashi Koenji Station, you'll find **U.F.O. Club** (1-11-6 Koenjiminami, Suginami-ku; map D4). This unassuming venue is a temple for acolytes of Japan's experimental noise-music scene and is known to host pioneers like Merzbow and recent experimenters Oshiripenpenz.

A few minutes' walk north of Higashi Koenji Station is one of Japan's most legendary venues, **Niman Denatsu** (1-7-23 Koenjiminami, Suginami-ku; map D4). This is the reincarnation of 20000V, a key venue in the formation of Japan's punk-rock community. After the original place was consumed by fire, the new Niman Denatsu (which literally means '20,000 Volts') took up the mantle in 2009.

Annual street-dance festival

Aside from counterculture, Koenji's other claim to fame is the Awa Odori, a heaving street-dance festival that takes place every year on the last weekend of August. Over a million people come to revel on the streets as teams perform the unique traditional dance of Tokushima Prefecture.

Take an afternoon walk along Yokohama's scenic waterfront

When people say 'Tokyo' they are usually referring to the world's largest conurbation, home to more than 30 million and an area that takes in the historic port city of **Yokohama**. By itself Japan's third-largest city by population, Yokohama has a flavour all of its own. It's just 30 minutes from central Tokyo and a worthwhile destination in its own right, particularly when combined with a visit to nearby Kamakura (see page 158).

Pages could be devoted to Yokohama, but when in town the must-sees begin and end at the waterfront. From the bayside you can amble over to nearby Chinatown and get stuck into a solid meal.

A good route is to begin at Sakuragicho Station and wander over to the **Yokohama Red Brick Warehouse**. This is a pair of western-style warehouses dating from the 1920s, when they made up the Customs Inspection House for Yokohama Bay. The buildings have been restored and converted into an attractive shopping centre housing 40 different shops, bars, cafés and restaurants. They're right on the water and afford great views of the Yokohama skyline on the bay.

Heading west, **Yamashita Park** is another popular spot from which to survey the harbour. Nearby are some old homes that were occupied by the first western traders in Japan, as well as Chinatown, formed by settlers who arrived as the port opened up, and now Japan's largest. For a meal, try **Shinkinko** for its atmospheric old building and quality Szechuan cuisine.

Yokohama Red Brick Warehouse; 1-1-2, Shinko, Naka-ku; tel: 045-211-1515; www.yokohama-akarenga.jp/en; Warehouse One 10am–7pm, Warehouse Two 11am–8pm, with individual shop variations; map D3
Shinkinko; 146 Yamashitacho, Naka-ku; tel; 045-663-1696; daily 11am–3pm and 5–10pm; map D3

Explore robot technology and cutting-edge research at the National Museum of Emerging Science and Innovation

Ride the futuristic, driverless Yuri-kamome elevated train to the artificial island of Odaiba, and you will find the fittingly striking **National Museum of Emerging Science and Innovation**. Hajime Narukawa's glass and steel building stands out for its protruding silver hemisphere. Step inside and find a giant globe called the Geo-Cosmos that uses 10,362 OLED panels to display near real-time global weather patterns, ocean temperatures and vegetation cover.

You could easily spend half a day at what locals simply call the *Miraikan* (Future Hall). Exhibitions, generally accompanied by good English explanations, are grouped around themes including space, the solar system, the future, the internet, robotics, the Earth and life.

Honda's walking, talking Asimo is the star of a popular show, while other robotics exhibitions present the latest in 'emotional' android robots that Japanese researchers are designing for therapeutic as well as commercial purposes.

Complete your trip with a visit to the museum's Dome Theater GAIA, a spherical theatre that screens 3D films including *The Man from the 9 Dimensions*, which guides viewers through the esoteric world of theoretical physics via live action scenes, mesmerising graphics and the latest scientific data-visualisation techniques.

National Museum of Emerging Science and Innovation; 2-3-6 Aomi, Koto-ku; 3570-9151; Wed–Mon 10am–5pm; map G1

More science museums
The **National Museum of Nature and Science** in Ueno emphasises the natural world, while the **Science Museum** near the Imperial Palace is strong on interactivity for kids.

ESSENTIALS

ADDRESSES

Tokyo is divided into 23 *ku* (wards), which are subdivided into *cho* (districts), then numbered *chome* (blocks). Addresses in Japanese start with the city, followed by ward name, then district, city block and building numbers. This order is reversed, however, when written in roman letters (the order used in this guide).

C

CHILDREN

Although Tokyo is short on public parks and playgrounds, the city is like a giant hi-tech theme park in which kids are rollercoastered about on futuristic trains and monorails, greeted by flashing screens at every turn. Tokyo's safety, its abundant and clean public toilets, and its many pharmacies for infant necessities also make it a good choice for families.

CRIME AND SAFETY

Tokyo is one of the safest cities in the world, but visitors shouldn't become too nonchalant. Although rare, pickpocketing and muggings do happen, as do worse crimes. Police boxes *(koban)* can be found in all neighbourhoods, often near the major train stations.

CUSTOMS

Non-residents entering the country are given a duty-free allowance of 400 cigarettes, three 760ml bottles of alcohol, 2oz of perfume and gifts the total value of which is less than ¥200,000. For more information, see www.customs.go.jp/english/summary/passenger.htm.

D

DISABLED TRAVELLERS

While there is a drive to provide more accessible hotels, tourist facilities and public transport for disabled travellers, Tokyo is not an easy place for limited-mobility people to get around. Useful, but outdated, information is available at http://accessible.jp.org.

E

EARTHQUAKES

Tokyo is notoriously susceptible to earthquakes. It is wise, therefore, to check the emergency exits in your hotel. In the event of a tremor, safety precautions include turning off any electrical or gas sources, opening exits, and standing or crouching under a sturdy door lintel or heavy table.

ELECTRICITY

The current in Tokyo is 100 volts AC, 50 cycles. American-style plugs with two flat pins are used. Adaptors and transformers are required if you come from countries like Britain where the voltage is 240.

EMBASSIES

Australia: 2-1-14 Mita, Minato-ku; tel: 5232-4111; http://japan.embassy. gov.au/tkyo/home.html.
Canada: 7-3-38 Akasaka, Minato-ku; tel: 5412-6200; www.japan.gc.ca.
UK: 1 Ichiban-cho, Chiyoda-ku; tel: 5211-1100; http://ukinjapan.fco.gov. uk.
US: 1-10-5 Akasaka, Minato-ku; tel: 3224-5000; http://tokyo.usembassy. gov.

EMERGENCY NUMBERS

Ambulance and Fire: 119; Police: 110; Japan Helpline: 0570 000 911.

H

HEALTH AND MEDICAL CARE

No vaccinations are required to enter Japan. Tap water is safe, and medical care is good. Hospitals and clinics with English-speaking staff include: Japanese Red Cross Medical Centre, 4-1-22 Hiro-o, Shibuya-ku; tel: 3400-1311; www.med.jrc.or.jp
St Luke's International Hospital, 9-1 Akashicho, Chuo-ku; tel: 3541-5151; www.luke.or.jp
Tokyo British Clinic, 2F Daikan-yama Y Building, 2-13-7 Ebisu-Ni-shi, Shibuya-ku; tel: 5458-6099; www.tokyobritishclinic.com
Tokyo Medical and Surgical Clinic, 2F 32 Shiba-koen Building, 3-4-30 Shiba-koen, Minato-ku; tel: 3436-3028; www.tmsc.jp

HOURS AND HOLIDAYS

Officially, business hours are Mon–Fri 9am–5pm, but office workers often stay later. Shops open through the week, usually from around 10am to 7 or 8pm; many are open Sundays and closed another day of the week. Most restaurants open at around 11.30am and take last orders at about 9.30pm. Museums often close on Mondays. Restaurants, department stores and museums usually open on public holidays.

Public holidays

1 Jan: New Year's Day
2nd Mon Jan: Coming of Age Day
11 Feb: Foundation Day
20–1 Mar: Spring Equinox
29 Apr: Showa Day
3 May: Constitution Memorial Day
4 May: Greenery Day
5 May: Children's Day
3rd Mon July: Marine Day
11 August: Mountain Day
3rd Mon Sept: Respect the Aged Day
23–4 Sept: Autumn Equinox
2nd Mon Oct: Health and Sports Day
3 Nov: Culture Day
23 Nov: Labour Day
23 Dec: The Emperor's Birthday

I

INTERNET

The internet can be accessed in most hotel rooms as well as airbnb accommodation, either via LAN cable or Wi-fi. Free Wi-fi spots are increasing but are still scarce compared to many Western cities.

L

LANGUAGE

With its three alphabets, Japanese is a notoriously difficult language to learn. However, as a spoken language, Japanese is relatively easy to pronounce, and when used even in a basic form will often be greeted by the locals with joy. English is not widely spoken, but many people will understand written English, and it can be useful to write down what you're trying to communicate.

LGBTQ TRAVEL

The LGBTQ community tends to keep a low profile in Japan, and do not promote themselves in Tokyo as much as they do in other international cities. However, Tokyo is fairly tolerant of alternative lifestyles, and has a thriving scene with a selection of clubs, events and support networks.

A useful online starting point is http://gayjapannews.com/index_english.htm.

M

MAPS

Tourist offices provide adequate maps of the city for free. For more detail, buy the indispensable *Tokyo City Atlas: A Bilingual Guide*, published by Kodansha. Google Maps also now includes comprehensive views and information on Tokyo.

MONEY

The Japanese yen (¥) is available in 1-, 5-, 10-, 50-, 100- and 500- yen coins and 1,000, 2,000, 5,000 and 10,000 notes. Money can be exchanged at banks and authorised exchangers. Many shops do not accept credit cards, so carry a reasonable amount of cash. Major credit cards and cash cards linked to Cirrus, PLUS, Maestro and Visa Electron networks can be used at post office and Seven Bank (located at 7-Eleven stores) ATMs.

POST

Post offices are open Mon–Fri 9am–5pm; some are also open Sat 9am–3pm. For English-language information about postal services, including postal fees, call 0570-046 111 or go to www.post.japanpost.jp/index_en.html.

T

TELEPHONES

Tokyo's area code is 03, but you don't need to dial this within the city. To dial Tokyo from the UK, dial 00 (international code) + 81 (Japan) + area code (minus the initial 0) + the number. To call overseas from Tokyo, dial 001-010 before the country code.

Public telephones take telephone cards, although some may accept ¥10 and ¥100 coins.

Mobile (cell) phones. NTT DoCoMo (www.ntt.com/personal/services/mobile/one/visitor/en/product.html) and SoftBank Mobile (www.softbank-rental.jp/e) allow visitors to use their own numbers and SIM cards with their 4G services, although you will need to rent or buy a phone in Japan. Alternatively, rent a phone or a SIM card with a Japan-based number at Narita and Haneda airports to use during your stay. Most mobile numbers begin with 090 or 080.

TIME ZONES

Tokyo (like the rest of Japan) is +9 hours GMT, +14 hours EST (New York) and +17 PST (Los Angeles). Japan does not have summer daylight-saving time.

TIPPING

Tipping is not practised in Japan. However, some restaurants do impose a 10 percent service charge.

TOURIST INFORMATION

Japan National Tourist Organisation (JNTO; 3-3-1, Marunouchi, Chiyoda-ku; tel: 3201-3331; www.jnto.go.jp; daily 9am–5pm) offers information on all of Japan as well as Tokyo. For city-specific details, visit the **Tokyo Tourist Information Centre** (1F Tokyo Metropolitan Government No. 1 Building, 2-8-1 Nishi-Shinjuku; tel: 5321-3077; daily 9.30am–6.30pm), also at **Haneda Airport** (International Terminal 2F; tel: 6428-0653; 24 hours daily) and in the Kesei line station at Ueno (tel: 3836-3471; daily 9.30am–6.30pm).

TRANSPORT

Arrival by air

New Tokyo International Airport (Narita; tel: 0476-348 000;

www.narita-airport.jp) is about 40 miles (66km) east of the city, and **Tokyo International Airport** (Haneda; tel: 6428-0888; www.tokyo-airport-bldg.co.jp/en) is 10 miles (15km) to the south. The city's two airports are usually referred to as Narita and Haneda. Most international flights arrive at Narita.

Narita Airport to the city

Taxi. This is the most expensive option and usually the slowest. The fare to Tokyo is ¥20,000–30,000, but it's no quicker than the bus.

Limousine bus. Frequent and comfortable airport limousine buses (tel: 3665-7220; www.limousinebus.co.jp/en) are much cheaper than taxis; they cost ¥3,100 to most central Tokyo locations.

Train. This is the fastest way to reach Tokyo. Stations for the two competing express services are found on the basement level of both terminal buildings: the **JR Narita Express** (tel: 3423-0111, www.jreast.co.jp/e/nex), which takes an hour to Tokyo Station and costs ¥3,020, and the **Keisei Skyliner** (www.keisei.co.jp), which runs to Tokyo's Ueno Station, stopping first at Nippori. It takes 36 minutes to Ueno, costing ¥2,220. Both the JR and Keisei lines offer cheaper but slower non-express train services to the city.

Haneda Airport to the city

Taxi. It should take about 30 minutes to central Tokyo by taxi, costing around ¥7,000; but beware of traffic congestion.

Train. Most people opt for the cheaper trains. Frequent services run from the Keihin Kyuko Station in the airport basement. The train takes about 20 minutes to Shinagawa Station and costs ¥400.

Monorail. The Tokyo Monorail connects Haneda with Hamamatsucho Station on the JR Yamanote line. It takes only 17 minutes and costs ¥490, but can be very crowded.

Limousine bus. An airport limousine bus service connects Haneda with central Tokyo. Fares start at ¥1,000, depending on which part of the city you are heading to. There is also a service from Haneda to Narita that takes about 75 minutes and costs ¥3,100.

Arrival by road

Expressways are of extraordinarily high quality. Like in Britain, the Japanese drive on the left. Highway tolls are high, making trains and buses generally more economical.

Japan has an excellent system of **inter-city buses**. They are a comfortable and cheaper alternative to the bullet train. Buses include destinations not covered by trains, and many services are direct. Night buses are the cheapest, but leave late and arrive early. Some of these are operated by Japan Railways; buy tickets at the Green Window offices at JR stations.

The main JR bus office, where services from Kyoto and Osaka arrive, is on the Yaesu (east) side of Tokyo Station.

Arrival by train

The majority of train lines entering Tokyo from major Japanese cities, whether regular or Shinkansen (bullet train), stop at Tokyo Station; some also arrive at Ueno, Shinagawa and Shinjuku stations. Day trips to places like Hakone usually involve taking a private (non-JR) line. Most of these connect with major JR terminals like Shibuya and Shinjuku stations.

Transportation within Tokyo

Subway. Tokyo's clean, safe and convenient subway – made up of the nine-line **Tokyo Metro** (www.tokyo metro.jp) and the four-line **Toei** (www. kotsu.metro.tokyo.jp) – is the fastest and most economical means of getting across town.

The two systems are fully integrated and run to precise schedules indicated on timetables posted at each station. Services run from 5am to 12.30am at intervals of 2–3 minutes during rush hours, with frequencies dropping to around every 5–10 minutes in off-peak periods. The frequency reduces slightly at weekends. All stations have a route map indicating fares for each stop near the ticket machines, usually in English.

Fares are regulated on a station-to-station basis, so if you cannot determine the fare required, just purchase the cheapest ticket available (¥170 for Tokyo Metro lines, ¥180 for Toei lines) at the ticket machine. Fare correction can be done on arrival.

Pasmo magnetic smart cards (www.pasmo.co.jp), good on any public transport line in Tokyo, can be bought at subway stations (¥500 deposit) and recharged when depleted. JR's Suica cards are similar, and both can be used on subways, trains and buses.

Trains. Above ground, **Japan Railways** (JR) operates a service as efficient as the subway, with equivalent frequency and operating hours (5am–1am) on commuter lines. Like the subways, the lines are colour-coded.

Buses. There are no English signs on Tokyo buses, but imminent stops are announced by a recorded voice. Passengers pay on entry, dropping the flat fare (¥210) into a box located next to the driver; there's a machine in the box for changing notes if you don't have the coins. Tourist information centres and hotels can give you bus maps with the major routes marked. Buses generally run 5.30am–midnight.

Ferry. Tokyo River Buses (tel: 5733 4812; www.suijobus.co.jp) offer a range of services down the Sumida River and across Tokyo Bay. Other routes include a cruise around Tokyo Harbour (45 min), past Rainbow Bridge to Kasai Sealife Park (55 min), and to the Shinagawa Aquarium (35 min). All boats depart from Hinode Pier, near Takeshiba Station on the Yurikamome line. Look out for the striking, sci-fi-esque *Himiko* vessel, designed by manga artist Leiji Matsumoto, which morphs into the floating bar Jicoo at night (www.jicoofloatingbar.com).

Taxis. Taxis are a convenient but pricey way of getting around. They are readily available on the streets, and at every major hotel and railway station. The standard flagfall in Tokyo is ¥700; anything other than short trips can run from ¥3,000 to ¥5,000. No tipping is expected.

Roads are narrow and traffic congestion is appalling at rush hour. Additionally, most taxi drivers don't speak English, so it helps to have your destination written down in Japanese. Recommended taxi operators are Hinomaru; tel: 3212 0505; www.hinomaru.co.jp/taxi and Nihon Kotsu; tel: 5755 2336; www.nihon-kotsu.co.jp/en.

Driving and car rental. Tokyo is not an easy place in which to drive. Except on the often crowded expressways, there are few road signs in romanised Japanese, and parking is always a problem. For getting out of town, it is usually faster to take public transport. If you do need to hire a car, try **Toyota Rent-a-Car** (http://rent.toyota.co.jp/eng), which has branches at the airports and across the city.

V

VISAS

Nationals of most Western countries do not need a visa for a short visit. On arrival, visitors are usually granted temporary visitor status, good for 90 days. Anyone wishing to extend their stay should visit the Tokyo Regional Immigration Bureau office (5-5-30 Konan, Minato-ku; tel: 5796 7112; www.immi-moj.go.jp/english/index.html).

INDEX

Experience Tokyo
Editor: Helen Fanthorpe
Author: Dan Grunebaum
Update Production: Apa Digital
Head of Production: Rebeka Davies
Picture Editor: Tom Smyth
Cartography: Carte
Photography: 4Corners Images 1, 4/5, 6,
8/9, 15, 24, 84, 134; Aflo/REX/Shutterstock
18L, 63; Akiko Yanagawa 96; Alamy 10,
41, 50, 52, 62, 83, 89, 94, 99, 111, 114,
116, 125, 128, 129, 138, 142, 148, 149,
154, 157; AWL Images 46, 118, 150, 159;
Chad Feyen & Brad Bennett 160; Chris
Stowers/Apa Publications 11, 13, 19R, 35,
139, 147, 164; Christian Kadluba 75; City
Foodsters 56, 61, 98; Fumie Suzuki/REX/
Shutterstock 140; Getty Images 16, 18R,
29, 32, 33, 36, 37, 43, 44, 51, 57, 59, 64, 68,
69, 93, 100, 106, 107, 117, 122, 123, 133,
143, 165; H.P.FRANCE S.A 101; htordsa
112; Hilton Hotels & Resorts 38; iStock 19,
21, 30, 39, 40, 79, 91, 131; James Hadfield
162; JNTO 73; Leonardo 113; Matono
Hiromichi/Omotenashi Nihonbashi 14;
Michael Saechang 156; Ming Tang-Evans/
Apa Publications 17, 60, 95, 102, 108; Musée
Du Chocolat Théobroma 80; Omotenashi
Nihonbashi 45; Public domain 90, 132;
Richard Hung 42; Satoshi Nagare 77;
Shutterstock 12, 17R, 53, 54, 71, 72, 76, 126,
127, 144, 145, 161; SuperStock 31, 55, 82, 97,
115; Sutton-Hibbert/REX/Shutterstock 109;
Takashi Hososhima 70; UPLINK 74; VOISIN/
PHANIE/REX/Shutterstock 130; Yuichi
Sakuraba 81; Yuichi Shiraishi 141
Cover: Shutterstock

Distribution
UK, Ireland and Europe
Apa Publications (UK) Ltd
sales@insightguides.com
United States and Canada
Ingram Publisher Services
ips@ingramcontent.com
Australia and New Zealand
Woodslane
info@woodslane.com.au

Southeast Asia
Apa Publications (SN) Pte
singaporeoffice@insightguides.com
Hong Kong, Taiwan and China
Apa Publications (HK) Ltd
hongkongoffice@insightguides.com
Worldwide
Apa Publications (UK) Ltd
sales@insightguides.com

**Special Sales, Content Licensing
and CoPublishing**
Insight Guides can be purchased in bulk
quantities at discounted prices. We can
create special editions, personalised
jackets and corporate imprints tailored to
your needs.
sales@insightguides.com
www.insightguides.biz

First Edition 2017

All Rights Reserved
© 2017 Apa Digital (CH) AG and
Apa Publications (UK) Ltd

Printed in China by CTPS

Contact us
Every effort has been made to provide
accurate information in this publication,
but changes are inevitable. The publisher
cannot be responsible for any resulting loss,
inconvenience or injury. We would appreciate
it it readers would call our attention to any
errors or outdated information. We also
welcome your suggestions; please contact
us at: hello@insightguides.com
www.insightguides.com

INSIGHT  GUIDES

Plan and book your tailor-made holidays at insightguides.com/holidays

---

Built for travellers who like to explore and experience their chosen destination in unique ways, **insightguides.com/holidays** connects you with our local travel experts, who will plan and customise your trip to your preferences.

Visit **insightguides.com/holidays** to view our wide selection of unique, customisable trips and book your next holiday.

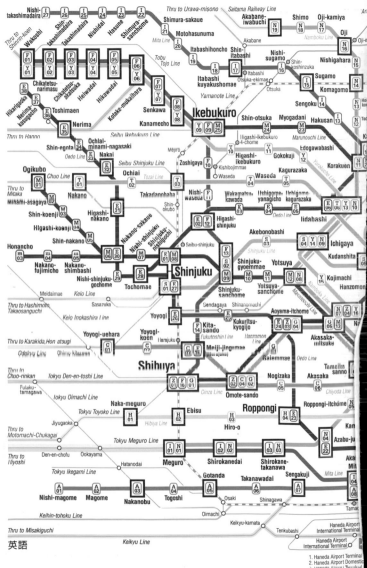
英語